Letters to America

Judaic Traditions in Literature, Music, and Art
Harold Bloom and Ken Frieden, *Series Editors*

Letters to
America

Selected Poems of **Reuven Ben-Yosef**

Edited and Translated by **Michael Weingrad**

Syracuse University Press

Copyright © 2015 by Syracuse University Press
Syracuse, New York 13244-5290

All Rights Reserved

First Edition 2015

15 16 17 18 19 20   6 5 4 3 2 1

∞ The paper used in this publication meets the minimum requirements
of the American National Standard for Information Sciences—Permanence
of Paper for Printed Library Materials, ANSI Z39.48-1992.

For a listing of books published and distributed by Syracuse University Press,
visit www.SyracuseUniversityPress.syr.edu.

ISBN: 978-0-8156-3398-3 (paperback)   978-0-8156-5325-7 (e-book)

Library of Congress Cataloging-in-Publication Data
Ben-Yosef, Re'uven, 1937–2001.
  [Poems. Selections]
  Letters to America : selected poems of Reuven Ben-Yosef / edited and
translated by Michael Weingrad. — First edition.
     pages cm
  Includes bibliographical references.
  ISBN 978-0-8156-3398-3 (pbk. : alk. paper) — ISBN 978-0-8156-5325-7
(e-book)
 I. Weingrad, Michael, editor, translator.   II. Title.
  PS3569.E4A6 2015
  811'.54—dc23   2015008000

Manufactured in the United States of America

Reuven Ben-Yosef was the author of eighteen volumes of Hebrew poetry and one volume of English poetry, two novels, two collections of essays, and a considerable number of translations. He was the recipient of several literary prizes, including Israel's Levi Eshkol Prize, the Jewish Book Council's Kovner Prize, and New York University's Neuman Prize for Hebrew Literature. Born in New York City in 1937, he immigrated to Israel in 1959 and served in the Israeli Defense Forces during the 1973 and 1982 wars. He died in Jerusalem in 2001 and is survived by his wife, his three children, and grandchildren.

Michael Weingrad is the author of *American Hebrew Literature: Writing Jewish National Identity in the United States*, published by Syracuse University Press in 2011. His essays have appeared in the *Jewish Review of Books*, *Commentary*, *Mosaic*, and other publications, and he writes regularly at the Investigations and Fantasies website. He is a professor of Jewish studies at Portland State University and lives in Oregon with his three children.

Contents

Acknowledgments

THIS PROJECT would not have been possible without the willingness of Reuven Ben-Yosef's family members to open their files and their homes, to help tell the story of Reuven/Robert, and to share their own stories as well. While the family tale I tell includes its share of strife, this volume is testament to the deep and evident love I witnessed and am privileged to chronicle. I cherish the conversations I had with Yehudit Ben-Yosef and with her children Tirzah, Carmi, and Naim. I regret that I have not yet had the opportunity to meet the poet James Reiss in person, but I am grateful for his impeccable suggestions regarding the manuscript, and for the humor and verve he lent to our correspondence. Wife, children, siblings: this family is formidable. I want to express my gratitude to them all.

I thank the editors and staff of Syracuse University Press for their diligence and patience, Ann Youmans for her fine copyediting, and the two anonymous readers of the manuscript for their helpful suggestions. Rabbi Tzvi Fischer answered my questions about rabbinic references in the poems, and Shaul Stampfer and Mel Berwin each lent their assistance during this project. As in such cases, my work has had the benefit of numerous and careful eyes. Errors are my own.

Esther Cameron, Curt Arnson, and Yehudit Ben-Yosef kindly allowed inclusion of several of their translations, some of which first appeared in *On The Bridge* (Bitsaron Press, 2011). Attribution in these cases is given in the notes on the poems.

Note on Translation

"POETRY," WRITES ELIOT WEINBERGER, "is that which is worth translating." My primary goal in translating this selection of poems by Reuven Ben-Yosef is to offer the English-language reader as vivid a sense as possible of the unique energy and feel of the poems in their Hebrew originals. I am not of the tribe of academic translators who insist the only way to do this is by rendering the Hebrew into dictionary-equivalent English and presenting the resulting oddities as proof of accuracy. There is a certain kind of fidelity in such cases, but it is not a fidelity to the actual experience of the poem, the way meaning, emotion, sound, and thought are deployed and received. So while I have certainly taken care to convey the literal meanings of Ben-Yosef's words and in many cases the same formal properties as the originals, I have also made use of cadences, affinities, and parallels in English that I hope impact the reader with the equivalent force of the originals in a way that would not happen had I opted for rigid word-by-word and foot-by-foot rendering at all times. Given the very divergent registers in which Ben-Yosef worked, I have also approached different poems in different ways. In each case and cumulatively, I have tried to earn the reader's trust: trust in the content, and trust in the overall experience of the poem.

Letters to America

Reuven Ben-Yosef and the Family Reiss

MICHAEL WEINGRAD

I am a pote [*sic*] and if I know one thing, it is poems and literarys.
But in Hebrew this is nothing. . . . I have no patience—I am used
to doing many daily things with language, I am used to writing
a lot, and to writing about things that are not simpel, and now
my wish—to work in language—is caught in prizin, like Joseph in
Egypt, solving the dreams but not going out of side to solve them
for real. (Ben-Yosef 1998, 7)

This passage is from an October 29, 1959, diary entry written by
Reuven Ben-Yosef. In my English translation, I've intentionally indi-
cated the errors of spelling and grammar in the Hebrew original,
which was written roughly seven months after he began learning
Hebrew, and a few weeks after his immigration from the United States
to the state of Israel. He was then twenty-two years old, twice the age
of his new country.

The passage is poignant. Clearly, this is someone accustomed to
excelling in language and literature, frustrated at the "prizin" of his
now limited abilities. Yet it also shows a man of impressive ability and
determination. Only a half a year after he first learned his *alef-bet*, and
a matter of days after arriving in Israel, he is able to keep a diary in
the language.

His progress continued to be impressive. He went on to transform
himself fully into a Hebrew writer, publishing eighteen volumes of
poetry, dozens of essays, and two novels in the language. Along the
way he won literary honors such as Israel's Levi Eshkol Prize and the

1

Bar-Ilan University Prize, and he translated numerous Hebrew writers into English, though never his own poems.

Reuven Ben-Yosef is not the only writer born and raised in the United States who then immigrated to Israel and made his literary career there. The body of American Israeli writing is various, including essayists, memoirists, and journalists such as Yossi Klein Halevi, Hillel Halkin, June Leavitt, Sherri Mandell, Adina Hoffman, Haim Chertok, Daniel Gordis, Haim Watzman, Aaron Wolf, Marcia Freedman, and Judy Lash Balint. Fiction writers include the novelists Naomi Ragen and Evan Fallenberg, the historian and former Israeli ambassador to the United States Michael Oren (who in addition to his magisterial works on Mideast history has also published novellas), and the bohemian suicide Alfred Chester. Poets of note include Shirley Kaufman, whose Israeli phase began in 1973 with her uncanny sequence of poems meditating on Henry Moore's elephant skull sketches and the Yom Kippur War; Robert Friend, for many years the main English-language poet in Israel; Peter Cole, also a distinguished translator of contemporary Arabic and medieval Hebrew poetry; and Gabriel Levin, whose father Meyer was the novelist who brought the Anne Frank diary to American shores.

All those I have mentioned are English-language writers, yet others, like Ben-Yosef, managed the daunting transition from English into Hebrew literature, in some cases to quite spectacular effect. This smaller group includes the writers T. Carmi, who grew up in a Hebrew-speaking household in the United States and so in some sense did not have to undergo a major linguistic upheaval; Harold Schimmel, whose playful New York School poetics, influenced by such poets as Frank O'Hara and George Oppen, have been so refreshing to the Israeli poetic tradition; and Jacob Jeffrey Green, better known as the translator of Aharon Apelfeld than as a fiction writer, though his 1998 novel *Sof-shavua ameriqani* (American weekend), set in western Massachusetts in the 1970s, is a fascinating snapshot of American and Jewish countercultural identities.

Among these writers, the literary life of Reuven Ben-Yosef stands as the most searingly moving portrait of the emotional costs, literary gains, and enduring tensions of the decision to leave the American promised land for the Jewish one. From the moment I began reading his poetry, above all the breathtaking poem "Mikhtavim la'Ameriqah" (Letters to America), I have been challenged, provoked, haunted, and inspired by this body of work and the man who produced it. I am addressed by these letters, both personally as a Jew drawn again and again to Israel yet living in what the medieval Hebrew poet Yehudah Halevy would call "the edge of the west" (in my case, Portland, Oregon) and as one of the five or six million Jews living today in the United States. I am convinced that because of the high literary quality of his work and the plangent calls he makes to his readers, his poetry demands both translation into English for its implicit American audience and reconsideration in Hebrew by its explicit Israeli audience. It is not the least of these poems' importance that they offer a new meeting ground for these two readerships.

I was not fortunate enough to have met Ben-Yosef before his untimely death in 2001. Yet I have had the pleasure of speaking with his siblings, his widow, and his children. As I explored his life and work, I came to see that his story is inevitably a family story, meaning both the family that he created in Israel and the parents and siblings he left behind in the United States. Ben-Yosef recreated himself in Israel and in Hebrew, yet he was never able fully to escape the influence of his American upbringing, a second star whose gravitational pull he alternately resigned himself to and struggled against savagely. His is simultaneously an Israeli story and an American story, in the subtly paradoxical sense of the two roads in the famous poem by Robert Frost, a poet he much loved, in which the decision to choose one path is fully meaningful only in light of the other, diverging from yet always dogging the first.

᷇

Reuven Ben-Yosef was born Robert Eliot Reiss in 1937 in New York City. His parents, Joseph and Cecilia, were proudly Americanized Jews. Cecilia's family had already been in the United States for two generations, her grandparents having emigrated from Galicia to New York in the 1850s, while Joseph's father had served in the Austrian army before coming to the United States at the end of the nineteenth century. After attending Columbia University, Joseph began working in advertising, and by dint of hard work and considerable struggle turned a small outfit into a successful firm with his younger brothers Harold and Ben before leaving it in order to run the lucrative Cecilia Cosmetics company he named after his wife.

Photographs of Robert, their first child, show a handsome little boy, with looks inherited from his glamorously beautiful mother and her Polish parents, Americanized in little Robert with his crew cut of sandy brown hair, broad smile, and precociously sculpted jaw. By contrast, his father, with dark, wiry hair, gaunt frame, and wan, pencil-thin moustache, resembled, despite his American business success, a haunted refugee from the Austro-Hungarian Empire. One also sees in Robert's childhood photographs a startling intensity of expression, as if his adult character, the will that would carry him from the United States to Israel and from English into Hebrew, were already fully formed. Indeed, Joseph felt bewildered by the force of his son's personality and the near-Oedipal intensity of his relationship with his equally dramatic mother. While Cecilia would loom large in Robert's life, his father, as if sensing from the start that he could not fill the patriarchal lineaments demanded by his son, seemed to withdraw from their relationship, leaving Robert ever hungry for a stronger male figure in his life.

Robert grew up in Manhattan, attending P.S. 187 and the High School of Music and Art before the family moved to New Jersey where he excelled as a student-athlete at Westwood High School in Bergen County. While he enjoyed sports, he was also a piano prodigy and, stirred by the bebop musicians of New York City in the early 1950s, shifted his focus at the age of fifteen from classical piano to jazz. As a teenager, he earned money playing piano in various nightclubs around the city and composed classical and jazz music. However, his creativity had yet to discover its proper channel, and while still in high school he began to exchange his musical pursuits for poetry.

He entered Oberlin College at seventeen, winning good marks and a place on the football team, and impressing the co-eds with his jazz piano skills. Yet he wanted the life experience he felt he needed as an aspiring writer, or at least more than he felt he could gain as an undergraduate, and so dropped out in his freshman year. Now subject to the draft, he was inducted into the U.S. army's intelligence division, sent to learn Russian in Monterey, and stationed for two years in West Germany. There he monitored Soviet troop broadcasts and saw his first poems in English published in the *New York Times*.

Two things happened in Europe which would define his life ever after. One was that Robert made contact with Jody, a girl whom he had dated briefly before dropping out of Oberlin, and who was spending her junior year abroad studying in England. Robert went to visit her on a brief leave in the summer of '57, and they quickly decided to get married. Rather than wait until his army service was done, in 1958 Jody withdrew from Oberlin and joined Robert in Germany.

The other pivotal event was that Robert became close friends with another young American soldier, also Jewish, an aspiring painter named Barry Fogelson. In the course of their conversations about art and literature, Barry sparked a heretofore nonexistent interest on Robert's part in his own Jewish heritage. Barry planned to join a kibbutz in Israel, and Robert became interested in following him there. However, at the end of 1958, Barry suddenly died of a kidney disease without ever having set foot in the Jewish state.

Robert and Jody decided to take up Barry's unfulfilled plan and immigrate to Israel themselves. Jody's family made no objection—her parents, in any case, had by then passed away. Robert's parents, on the other hand, were absolutely opposed to his making aliyah. Joseph and Cecilia had moved to the New Jersey suburbs where they attended an appropriately tony and liberal Unitarian church. They saw no reason to maintain a Jewish identity in a sophisticated and modern world. Israel seemed to them an atavistic ghetto. Cecilia's response to Robert's intention to move to Israel was to try to convince him to see the family psychiatrist. Nevertheless, Robert and Jody were set on their plan. They spent a final year in New York City, where they began learning Hebrew, and celebrated their first and last Passover in the United States.

And so, Robert Eliot Reiss left New York City, then the cultural and financial capital of the world, and precisely at the time of the great ascendance of Jewish writers and intellectuals as the new arbiters of American culture. In 1959 Phillip Roth unforgettably described the Jewish march into nouveau-riche suburbia in "Goodbye, Columbus," Saul Bellow hit the best-seller list with *Henderson the Rain King*, Allen Ginsberg prodded the embers of the old Jewish Left in "Kaddish," and Norman Mailer advertised himself.

That year Robert changed his first name to Reuven and his surname to Ben-Yosef, honoring the father who opposed the implications of such a name change. Jody, who was not Jewish and had grown up in a Midwestern Quaker family, converted to Judaism and changed her name to Yehudit. Their ship arrived at the port of Haifa on the eve of the Jewish New Year.

∛

In 1959, Israel had a total population of just over 2 million, its Jewish population the world's third largest after the United States and the Soviet Union. The few hundred immigrants from the United States of whom Ben-Yosef and his wife were two were a tiny drop in the stream of tens of thousands of Jews who arrived in Israel in the second half of the 1950s, many of whom were fleeing Communist oppression in Poland, Hungary, and Rumania and Pan-Arabist persecution in Egypt. In 1959 the country was contending, much as it is today, with the belligerence of its neighbors. Shelling and machine-gun fire across the northern border from Syria were common, and infiltrators crossed into Israel from Gaza to lay mines. Egypt enforced a boycott, not only of Israeli shipping through the Suez Canal but of Israeli cargo on other countries' vessels, which was often seized and confiscated.

In 1959, Tel Aviv celebrated its half-centennial. The author S. Yizhar won the Israel Prize for *Days of Ziklag*, his epic novel of the War of Independence. A record high of 92,000 tourists visited the country. Elections for the Knesset were held in November. The Labor Party under David Ben-Gurion increased its number of seats by seven, and cabinet positions were extended to up-and-coming younger party leaders such as Moshe Dayan and Shimon Peres. Ethnic tensions broke out in the Wadi Salib riots in which poor Moroccan Jews attacked the Haifa police. In 1959, the Israeli secret service began surveillance of a German living in Buenos Aires under the name of Ricardo Clement, suspected and later confirmed to be SS officer Adolf Eichmann.

From the port in Haifa, Reuven and Yehudit were taken to their new home, a kibbutz in the northern Galilee close to the Lebanese and Syrian borders. Kibbutz Hagoshrim (the bridge builders), so named because it is situated near the Snir and Dan rivers, was founded in the 1940s by Turkish Jews and affiliated with the socialist United Kibbutz movement. Reuven arrived with a minimal Hebrew vocabulary and a stubborn refusal to let a single word of English pass his or his wife's lips. "It was a rather quiet first year," Yehudit would later recall.

He was followed to Israel by the evidence of his short career as an English-language poet. *The Endless Seed*, published in 1959 under his original name by the Exposition Press in New York, was his first and last collection of poems in English. Copies reached him at Hagoshrim after he had already left the language for good.

It is difficult to assess a poetic career in the English language based on one book of poems written before the age of twenty-two, yet I can't help but wonder what Ben-Yosef's literary development might have been had he continued in English, just as I can't help but wonder what his life might have looked like had he remained in the United States. Certainly nothing in the slim volume comes close to matching the quality of his work in Hebrew. Its twenty-nine poems are classical in impulse and form, beginning with an elegy and ending with an epithalamium, avoiding free verse for sonnets and rhymed stanzas. They wear with heavy seriousness the influences of Spenser, Donne, and Shakespeare, with glints, among the moderns, of Frost and Crane, who would haunt him into the beginning of his Hebrew career. Most of the poems are competent, none are excellent, though potential is everywhere apparent.

Jewish references are all but absent in this book, the exceptions being biblical in theme and confined to a sequence of poems treating Robert's decision to move to Israel through the imagery of the

Exodus, and one other poem bearing the title "Cain and Abel." There is not a hint in any of the other poems that the author is Jewish or has ever pondered matters such as Israel, Jewish life, anti-Semitism, or the Holocaust. The absence of the last is particularly notable, given his time spent in Germany. "Peace in 1956," one of a half-dozen poems that first appeared in the *New York Times,* refers to World War II only to reflect on the subsequent Cold War. The instructive and partial exception to this absence of Jewish themes is the sequence that begins with "The Burning Bush," a poem about God's call to Moses and obviously resonant with Robert's own awakening to Jewish consciousness. The poem registers an ineluctable command that brings Moses from "layman's indecision" to the "fact" of national belonging, yet this "fact" is rather abstract—"out of vagueness came / The huge concretion" (1959, 31)—or perhaps loomed so large and so self-evidently for the poet that he found it difficult to articulate.

More helpful in understanding what drove Ben-Yosef to Israel is the first poem in that collection, "The Artists Mourn Barry Fogelson." Here, Ben-Yosef presents his dead friend as a failed artist-redeemer, someone who, had he not died young, could have effected a kind of cultural restoration based on two principles. First, there must be a return in art and literature to the values of western classicism, which nourish the human and defend against the nihilisim and alienation of both modern life and modernist art. Second, the artist must be rooted in a community rather than a solitary figure. In the poem, the "artists," speaking in the plural, mourn Barry Fogelson—"Blackness is our seed now, and our spring" (1959, 11), they lament—creating the Lycidas-like illusion that Fogelson was already the laureled bard of some pastoral nation, whereas in reality the poem describes only the impact of one young, unknown painter upon one young, unknown poet. It seems to have been Fogelson's conviction, and subsequently Robert's, that the return to classical values must be instantiated in an organic community where art can be the product of a nation, nourishing its artists and nourished by them, rather than the expression of atomized individuals as seemed to be the case in the United States.

Years later, in the autobiographical novel *Haderekh hazarah* (The Way Back), Ben-Yosef elaborated these ideological convictions, describing in his conversations with Fogelson their rejection of modernism for classicism and their hope to join a society in which the artist and his people would be united in an organic relationship—all of which Robert and Barry believed they would find on the kibbutzim of Israel. "I think that if I belonged to a place like that," the Fogelson character in the novel says, "I would know the people there and, since I would live among them, I would paint them and offer my painting for their enjoyment. Like in Florence in the days of Michelangelo" (1973, 60–61).

Looking for Renaissance Italy on a kibbutz is a recipe for disappointment, yet the critique of western modernity that we see here was not entirely uncommon among American writers, artists, and intellectuals throughout the twentieth century and certainly on the eve of the 1960s. In any case, we see that Robert's impulse to move to Israel was as much an artistic-social vision as any kind of political one. It was a wish to join the Jewish nation as a national poet, and this would have considerable ramifications for his subsequent career. As for English, he did write a final literary composition in the language in the last months before he left for Israel. This never-published verse play treats the biblical Exodus from the perspective of an Egyptian family, emphasizing the tragic inability of the parents' generation to break away from their hollow society and follow their children into freedom.

⤸

Ben-Yosef's attempt to transform himself in his twenties from an English poet into a Hebrew one was a difficult struggle. Turning again to his writer's diary, we find numerous despairing passages such as this one from June 1961: "Here I am, an adult in years and so poor in tongue," he writes. "How will I write in this language?" He complains anxiously, "If I had continued in English I would have already created work of some significance. Will I do so in Hebrew?" (1998, 13). In December 1965, he describes his worry that he "will never graduate" in his new language. "Six years," he writes. "I'm trying to build a life on six years. I'm a six year old, but without first grade and so unable to study; without childhood's freedom and so unable to learn unencumbered by responsibility; without a mother and so unable to cry" (69).

Nevertheless, Ben-Yosef's linguistic progress was striking. By the spring of 1961, he reports (in Hebrew, naturally) to friends, "I'm keeping to my program of study in Bible, Aggadah [rabbinic legends], and modern literature. I've already nearly finished Genesis, but reading Mendele [a foundational late nineteenth-century writer] goes more slowly" (10). A couple of months later, he is on to Exodus and is reading the modern prose writers Agnon and Brenner. In October, he is reading the biblical Isaiah and moderns Tchernikhovsky and Hazaz. "Now I'm beginning to deal not only with the Hebrew language," he reflects, "but also with its poetry . . . I want to explore these materials and tools and know them as a carpenter knows wood and saw" (16). At the beginning of 1963, he had read most of Haim Nahman Bialik's poetry, Ezekiel, and Psalms and was intensively engaged in the works of twentieth-century poets such as Shin Shalom, Uri Zvi Greenberg, and Yehuda Karni. In short, he worked his way methodically through the classical Hebrew literary tradition, from the Bible through the nineteenth-century Revival, often memorizing entire chapters of the former and whole poems from the latter.

In his acquisition of literary Hebrew, Ben-Yosef credited one person above all. Frumke Eshed was a veteran member of the famous kibbutz at nearby Ein Harod and a beloved teacher in the kibbutz world. Born in a small town near Vilna in 1895, she left home at the age of twelve to work in a factory in Warsaw where she became friendly with Yiddish writers such as Kadya Molodowsky and I. J. Singer. In 1923, she immigrated to Palestine. She and her husband Yaakov, a respected writer, editor, socialist theoretician, and leading activist in the United Kibbutz movement, became something like substitute parents for Ben-Yosef. They were the socialist-Zionist mother and father he never had, state-building pioneers after whom Ben-Yosef sought to model himself, and they also provided a direct connection to the world of eastern Europe that was only a distant memory in his American family. Moreover, since they had spent several years in the late 1940s as *shlihim* (overseas representatives) in the United States, they had experienced firsthand what Ben-Yosef had rejected in moving to Israel, sharing his ideological conviction that the assimilating American Jewish community was a tragic loss to the Jewish people. "If one can say that we were born anew in our immigration," Ben-Yosef wrote to the Esheds in August 1964, "then you are our parents and our educators in this new life" (43).

It was Frumke who responded to the immigrant's desire to become a Hebrew writer and who recognized the iron discipline that would allow him to do so if provided the right instruction. For several months in the winter of 1960–61, she therefore transformed a kibbutz shack into a kind of laboratory in which Ben-Yosef spent his days in study of Bible and Hebrew literature, the materials he saw as necessary to become a poet in his new language (see the poem "In the Room Where I Studied"). The experiment was a success. In 1962 he began publishing his first poems in Hebrew, and in 1965 his first collection in Hebrew, *Shehafim mamtinim* (Waiting Gulls), was published by the prestigious publishing house Hakibutz Hameuhad. He dedicated the book to Frumke.

While slim at fifty pages, *Waiting Gulls* is an impressive debut in Hebrew letters. Half of the volume is taken up by the long poem "Ha'ir" (The City), written in 1964 and based partly on the experience of Ben-Yosef's first visit back to the United States since his immigration, a few months after the birth of his daughter Tirzah in May 1962. New York City was fraught territory for him, the antithesis of his life at Hagoshrim, and he bristled with resistance to his parents' bourgeois, American way of life. In a letter to the Esheds, he refers to New York as *nekhar* (1998, 19)—a foreign land—and describes the city as if it were the demonic metropolis in Eliot's *The Waste Land* or Bialik's "Yenaser lo kilvavo." "The heavens are dark yet no rain falls," he tells the Esheds. "And yet we know that even if it rained, no flower would bud, no grass would spring up from the thick stone of the sidewalk. Tall buildings block out the sun, covering the entire sky."

He chafes at the luxury of his parents' home, where "in a wealthy, electrified mansion our souls weep over those simple things we've left behind" (19).

The poem's cantos present twelve different episodes. It begins with his airplane's descent over Manhattan with a view of the nearby Statue of Liberty, runs through various city scenes—a ride on the subway, a visit to a watch repair shop, a trip to the zoo, sections on his mother and father—and ends with the plane's departure for the return journey to Israel. As he wrote in his diary during the poem's composition: "I only want to express the essence of the emotion. The images are realistic, but the overall environment is imaginary" (1998, 36). He conveys this emotion-landscape not through metaphor—"I want to offer the city itself" (37), he claimed—but by condensing real images and charging them with uncanny intensity, more visionary than symbolic. The landscape of the present—say, a subway ride—is everywhere shot through with childhood:

> A train underneath highway and river,
> as a boy I stayed here rocking,
> to no station: the passengers
> continually being born and dying, and my birth carried on
> among the familiar walls, always
> new in the dark. (1965, 36)

The poem's intentional restlessness, nervousness, is carefully sculpted from its six-line unrhymed and irregularly metered stanzas. On the one hand, the idiom is the closest he would ever come to a high Anglo-American modernism, resembling Eliot especially when he is most negative about the urban landscape, and even more under the sway of Crane's *White Buildings*. On the other hand, Ben-Yosef sought his models for raising the image to the level of vision in biblical prophets such as Ezekiel and Zechariah, and in modern Hebrew writers such as Bialik, Shin Shalom, and (in Hebrew translation) the Yiddish writer Moyshe-Leyb Halpern.

New York City in the poem is a painful love, a seductive yet ever unavailable woman, an Oedipal mother figure, the American childhood Reuven left behind but that haunts him. She is the Statue of Liberty in the first canto: "a desired woman, her head turned away unresponding." Rather than castigating as in his letters from 1962, Reuven portrays his ambivalent emotions about the city, desire and fear, the child's hunger for a mother's approval and the spurned lover's craving for an unavailable woman. The poem concludes,

> You did not come near, you did not respond, you did not listen
> to the scrape of my nails on the walls, I go up to the plane,
> in bridges of light after light you are extinguished.
> I'm already awake, will I hear your name again?
> In the gossip of leaves,
> or in a star's lullaby. (1965, 49)

He had written, when composing the poem, "It is important that there be a clear progression of mood, a clear line leading to the awareness that there is no returning to the city" (1998, 37). The poem, however, shows that there is no fully escaping it, either.

Of any of his books, *Waiting Gulls* carries the loudest echoes of American poetry. Hart Crane's poem "My Grandmother's Love Letters" whispers in the corners of the section translated from "Kishnei prahim batsiah" (Like Two Flowers in the Desert). Dickinson presides over "Baheder bo lamad'ti" (In the Room Where I Studied). Frost is audible in others. Yet Ben-Yosef was thrilled when the labor leader Yitzhak Tabenkin pronounced of the book, "Here is something new, and it is all Hebrew, very Hebrew" (1998, 54).

As "The City" indicates, Ben-Yosef's rebirth into a new language did not mean that he had resolved his relationship to his American past. Nor was he fully secure in his place in his Israeli present. Anticipating a visit from his parents in the fall of 1966, for instance, he wrote to the Esheds about his ongoing struggles with "the old world that seeks at all costs to hold on to me and thwart my forward progress" (84). He confided,

> In every positive thing that I've tried to do here in Israel it seems
> that I fight the habits of my past, the customs and conventions of

13

my childhood. . . . The image of my parents returns me to a place so distant that it's difficult to believe it's me . . . the difficulty being one of anger and tears. And even now when I can assume that I have succeeded in saving myself and my children for the sake of the future, my parents are still left in the far-off world that fights us.

He reported a few weeks later that, despite his fears, the visit was pleasant. Joseph and Cecilia showed up with a dozen suitcases full of toys for the children and expensive gifts for Reuven and Yehudit, including a movie camera. "I wanted to run away" (85), Reuven told the Esheds, as his parents' largesse washed over his spartan kibbutz existence, but he appreciated their gifts all the same and, even more, their new willingness to witness the life that he and Yehudit had made for themselves in Israel.

But it was not only his wealthy American parents who were out of sync with the kibbutz ethos. Ben-Yosef's expectations of what kibbutz life would be like were doomed to be disappointed, and the collision with reality was painful. Although he moved to Israel believing that he would find on the kibbutz a new, distinctively Jewish national culture that would embrace him and nurture his artistic potential, at Hagoshrim he had to fight for months with the kibbutz secretariat to be permitted even one day a week away from agricultural work in order to write. He found the socialist, collectivist ethos of the kibbutz oppressive; it brought out a very American desire for precisely the individual freedom and privacy he had rejected in order to move to Israel. In a letter to Yaakov Eshed written in November 1963, Ben-Yosef expressed tremendous frustration with the pressure to conform to the accepted way of life on the kibbutz, the "constant criticism," the denial of individual autonomy. "The kibbutz must decide if it is ready to acknowledge human difference," he wrote, "or if it wants to make each person exactly equal and identical to the next" (1998, 30). On the one hand, he persisted through the 1960s in believing that the kibbutz was "the last refuge, the last hope that it might be possible to activate the positive characteristics in mankind to arrive at creation, at the good." On the other hand, this was a theory that he never found borne out in reality. He felt attacked for his habits, his opinions, the way in which he and Yehudit raised their children. He wrote to Yaakov that "the most destructive force" arrayed against him as a writer was the "duty to be 'social.'"

In 1964 the family moved to another kibbutz, Cabri, near Nahariyah, and after several years he was granted a full three days of writing and study time during the week. Yet he still found kibbutz life intolerable. He tried to obtain a post as a cultural emissary to the United States, which would have allowed him to advocate Zionist immigration among young American Jews, but the plan came to nothing when his sponsor at the overseas agency left her position. In 1968 he and Yehudit had had enough, and they moved to Tel Aviv. Ben-Yosef was especially conscious of having disappointed the Esheds but explained to Frumke, who died later that year, "I've dedicated to you much more than my first book." To stay on the kibbutz would be "to sacrifice myself for you" (127).

∾

In 1967, Ben-Yosef's second collection of poems, *Derekh erets* (The Way of the Land) was published, also by Hakibutz Hame'uhad, and was followed by *Ka'asher at mitlabeshet* (As You Get Dressed) in 1969 and *Metim ve'ohavim* (The Dead and the Loving) in 1974. Each of these collections has its high points and leaps beyond the previous in terms of ambition. Yet this progression cannot be described in terms of mere "improvement," as if Ben-Yosef began as a crude and unskilled poet and got more refined as he went. His first collection in Hebrew, *Waiting Gulls*, already contains technically accomplished, gorgeous, perplexing, and touching poems. Ben-Yosef was too devoted to poetry to publish these books before he had the skill to write the poems he wanted to write. While there is technical development in Ben-Yosef's poetry over the course of the 1960s and into the 1970s, the more noticeable development is the emergence of an increasingly sure and sustained "lyric self" in Hebrew—a speaking subject we recognize and respond to as a thinking, feeling individual. Such a unified presence does not exist in these first collections, nor was it a necessary ingredient for the major poems he wrote during that period. Yet it would be necessary for his major poems of the 1970s, and one notices both the superb and dazzling poems in his first books while also the gradual coming into being of the voice one hears later on.

One also notices several thematic threads running through these early books, such as Ben-Yosef's imaginative preoccupation with geological, evolutionary, and cosmogonic processes, from the creation of new islands to the death of stars. In the poem "Behikasef" (What Was Longed For), he places his erotic desires in a vast evolutionary context, beginning with

> silent cells,
> then worms crawl from the sea
> to warm themselves, and after a billion years: birds. . . . (1969, 9)

In the sequence "Badimdumim" (At Twilight), he mixes images of the catastrophe of the biblical Flood with creation from the primeval mud, casting himself as both an Adam (with Yehudit as his Eve) and a Noah whose solitude is not that of the first man but rather the sole survivor of a deluge. The poem "In Memory of My Living Parents" also reprises the account of life on earth from amoebae to dinosaurs to *Homo sapiens*:

> man was created
> like a star, his strength was wrenched from cosmic fire
> to freeze as formless rock until the coming
> of water, life, coral cells, seaweed
> climbing toward the air, the mighty lizard
> that chews the trees like cud, the apes too tired
> to jump, the rocks in the hands of men that swarm,
> multiplying in my memory, in your sighs,
> Father, and, Mother, in your endless tears. (1969, 38–39)

The poem then imagines a reunion with his parents that is darkly ironic because it is accomplished through annihilation, in nuclear destruction ("uranium, plutonium, / exploding, wiping out at a single blow / the past") or perhaps in the death-throes of a supernova:

all of us united, as the whole earth
turns into heaven, and my poems and what's left
turns imaginary as the voices of stars. . . . (39)

Another thematic development is the introduction of the Holocaust into the literary landscape of his memory. As mentioned, Ben-Yosef was largely indifferent to the reality of the Holocaust when he lived in Germany, but after his arrival in Israel the implications of his previous lack of awareness would become occasional themes of his poetry, sometimes darkening the poetic recollection of his youth in the United States and Germany, as when he writes, in the long sequence "A Night and Day of Love," of

bridges of smoke to there, where my desire
and laughter gather on ashen flags;
and the rustle of white dresses behind the ruined
wall, and rats squeaking in the rosebushes. (1967, 62)

Later, this theme would be taken up more explicitly, as in the several poems in this collection that refer to the poet Yitzhak Katznelson, who was murdered in Auschwitz.

A third element in these books is Ben-Yosef's periodic return to the figure of his friend Barry Fogelson, the catalyst for his immigration and inspiration for his artistic quest. As noted, his elegy to Fogelson was the major poem in his first published collection in English. A decade later, he returned to the theme in his second book in Hebrew, in a similarly ambitious sequence, "Lezikhro shel Bari Fogelson" (In Memory of Barry Fogelson), that develops the conceit of death, decay, and rebirth in the natural cycle of moist and rotting forests in order to reassure the poet that Fogelson may be resuscitated in memory. A third poem, though, published seven years after the second, avoids the agricultural metaphors of the first and the lush woodlands of the second to end with the blue-purple spines of the dry, wild, magnificently ubiquitous Israeli globe thistle:

I remember your life and I pass through
the hardness of summer in the land you wanted

so much to come to, and through winter days
that waver in mist and pass away
like winter days. And I am reminded of nothing
but next year's narcissus,
and cyclamen, and on to the globe thistle,
to the blue thorn of the beginning of memory. (1974, 9)

This becomes the true acknowledgment that Fogelson could never really be part of Ben-Yosef's life in Israel, that there is, finally, no metaphor to carry the artist to "the land you wanted / so much to come to," only Ben-Yosef's memories, stubborn, spiky things. In the end, he seems to say, one receives only what the untamed land gives, not what one plants and cultivates.

❧

The next major phase in Ben-Yosef's literary career was inaugurated by the traumatic and transformative experience of the 1973 Yom Kippur War. Ben-Yosef had been inducted into the Israeli military in 1965, a step that at the time required him to forfeit his American citizenship. Despite numerous petitions to be placed in a combat unit, he was not called into action during the Six Day War of 1967 and he spent that period on extra work shifts in the banana fields of his kibbutz. Neither able to take time off to write nor to fight on the front, he felt like a bystander in a country that seemed to have little use for him, and we find no record in his writings of the great fear felt by most Israelis as the Egyptian army massed on the southern border in May and June of that year. We likewise find neither messianic exhilaration nor military triumphalism in his poems and writings in the wake of Israel's extraordinary victory. His sequence of poems "Incidental War: 1967" reflects only the relief of soldiers at the war's end and the sorrow of a war widow, and it begins sardonically with the stated intention to write war poems neither overly aesthetic nor academic—that is, poems

Without rhyme, such as "eyes"
And "At the machine gun / Number two will
go on, if number one dies."

A book all readers can understand,
poetic lines with no metre at all,
unlike the soldiers that fall. (1967, 31)

He wrote to the Esheds in August 1967, "I don't believe—and here I seem to differ from the public at this time—that our recent victory has granted us the redemption for which generations have yearned," continuing,

It's good that we won, mainly because by doing so we avoided losing, and it's preferable to live than to die, even for a Jew. I'm kidding of course: it's better especially for a Jew.

But redemption? That is an indescribable fulfillment, and the way toward it isn't through war with the Arabs.

(1998, 116)

Ben-Yosef was assigned to a combat unit the following year, and trained as a gunner in an armored vehicle unit. He served frequently in the Sinai and in Gaza during the long War of Attrition carried on by Egypt in the wake of the Six Day War, documenting the experiences in poems such as "Gaza Like Death."

The war that left the deepest mark on Ben-Yosef, both personally and in his poetry, began with the surprise attack by Egypt and Syria on the Day of Atonement in 1973. Ben-Yosef and his wife and young children were camping on Mount Meron when a Syrian fighter jet came roaring over their heads. When they realized what was happening, Yehudit hurried home with the children while Reuven rushed to join his unit. He didn't return home for five months, serving in the grueling counterattacks that at great cost drove the Syrian army back from the Golan. From these experiences came profound and acerbic poems such as "On the Basalt of the Golan Heights" and "On the Eternal Mission" in his 1976 collection *Qolot baRamah* (Voices in Ramah). The Golan Heights in many poems become Ben-Yosef's new Sinai, delivering commandments that he can hardly keep:

thou shalt not scream when a kid
sobs over his dead friend, hugging

his weapon and gazing heavenward
as if he knows that the chopper will come
rising from the Galilee, and from the hilltop
they alert your vehicle that the enemy is back,
two tanks in front of your slender cannon. (1989, 118)

It was in this war that Ben-Yosef shared most deeply in the trauma and sacrifice of the nation as a whole, achieving in war a connection to his country that he had not yet found in his career as a poet. For the rest of his life, he would return to this war in his poetry as a kind of touchstone for his questions about the fate and destiny of the Jewish people and his own role within that story. "Ten years since the Yom Kippur War," he writes in the reflective little poem "Ten," watching his youngest son riding his bike during the Days of Awe (the period leading up to Yom Kippur) and pondering as soldier and as father the connection between Jewish chosenness and Jewish suffering. In response to another child asking why there are ten commandments, he wonders,

what would my answer be
on these days of repentance beneath a mild sun,
on a bench in the neighborhood, and my son riding
back and forth grasping the handlebars
with his ten fingers. (1989, 288)

∽

Ben-Yosef's finest poetic creation, and one of the best long poems written by any Israeli poet of his generation, was shaped less by the national crisis of the Yom Kippur War than by a personal crisis: the breakdown of family relations that took place in the war's aftermath. Towards the end of the war, Ben-Yosef's mother Cecilia had come to Israel. His father Joseph had died three years earlier, and she thought she might move permanently to Israel to be with her son. Instead, her long-standing emotional instability and the fraught family dynam-ics reasserted themselves with a vengeance. She cursed Ben-Yosef, declaring that he would die before she did, and returned to America.

Meanwhile, he and his brother and sister had drifted apart, and he was unsuccessful even in contacting them when his third child was born in 1976.

This makes up the immediate background to the composition of "Mikhtavim la'Ameriqah" (Letters to America), written primarily in February 1977 but already commenced in 1974. "This work has possibly been harder than anything I've done till now," he wrote during its composition. "I only hope that the result justifies the effort, the pain connected with the core subject" (1998, 167). The poem is blisteringly confessional, excoriating his family members in a series of "letters" that, as none of them could read Hebrew, would never really arrive. They indict his brother for his ensconcement in the United States, his mother for her abandonment of her son and Israeli grandchildren, his sister for her betrayal of Judaism in her marriage out of the faith. They address his brother's daughters and even the children his sister never had, yearning wistfully for a "rescue" of this assimilating generation by bringing them to Israel. The poem explores his own childhood in New York, family trips to Florida, his decision to emigrate, the shadow of the Holocaust, and the trauma of the Yom Kippur War. It refers periodically to, and concludes with, his father's death, cremation, and the scattering of his ashes in the Atlantic Ocean off the coast of Florida:

> My father is not here. He is in the Diaspora,
> dispersed in every river and ocean.
> In the seas and the lakes. In wood. In stone.
> My father who yearned to sail the waves,
> and finally did. (1978, 53)

The poem is saved from what might have been an unrelievedly hectoring brutality by both its emotional complexity and its literary brilliance. The latter derives from the poem's dazzling combination of allusions to biblical and classical Jewish texts, wordplay, and powerful cadence, all of which I hope my translation gives some analagous sense. To take one example from just one line, look at poem 7, addressed to Ben-Yosef's nieces, presented as assimilated Jews living in

New York City. The poem plays throughout on the Song of Songs, as Ben-Yosef declares he is no typical American "rich uncle"—*dod ashir* in Hebrew—but more like the *dod bashir*—the beloved in the biblical song, searching for his nieces who are "lost" to the New York Christmas season, just like the woman in the Song of Songs who searches for her lost lover (1978, 58). Or, to take another example, in the final poem, when he recounts throwing his father's ashes into the ocean, he writes that

> some of my parents' acquaintances
> borrowed a motorboat from the locals,
> the kind of boat I wanted as a boy,
> that could cut across the sea. But this time it was clear
> that one can't go far with borrowed vessels. (70)

The bitter pun here is on the borrowed vessels, both the rented motorboat but also (as the Hebrew makes clear) a reference to the gold and silver items the Israelites borrowed from the Egyptians and took with them on their exodus. This time there would be no splitting of the sea and journey to the promised land: the family would stay in their American exile.

The poem's emotional complexity is felt in the unexpected and poignant register of vulnerability and need that runs through it. Ben-Yosef is not simply delivering a Zionist lecture to his family: he desperately wants their approval (as son, brother, poet), their love, and their closeness. His own name, "son of Joseph," and the references in the "Letters" to his father's biblical namesake inevitably draw in the biblical story's focus on family strife, betrayal, exile, and tearful reunion. Moreover, the poem is not only a confessional exercise. Ben-Yosef referred repeatedly in his diary to the series as *hapo'emah al yahadut Ameriqah*—the poem about American Judaism (or American Jewry). That is, he clearly did not mean for the poem to be limited to a set of literal or confessional addresses to specific family members—who, again, could not and apparently were never meant to read them. And, while the poems clearly have their specificity, they also depart in some details from biographical fact, swerving into a kind of mythology. In short, the power of the poems is not as an address to a few individuals but in their greater symbolic resonance as an address—imploring, furious, wounded, loving—to American Jewry as a whole. This makes "Letters to America" the epicenter of Ben-Yosef's oeuvre, the dark lament and litany of complaint by the American Israeli, who, in the wake of the Yom Kippur War and the tumultuous shifts in Israel, and with the shadow of the Holocaust darkening his childhood memories, wants not only his own family but all American Jews to join him:

> And it is important to write letters to America.
> Because 6 million Jews are there, less one,
> 6 million alive, more or less like the number
> consigned to the flames in my childhood
> far from the old, forgotten world, led to their deaths
> in railway cars while I as a boy played on the wall-
> to-wall carpet with electric trains, the gift of my father. (53)

❧

Ben-Yosef was guided in his writing by several aesthetic principles, some conscious and intentional, others less so. One that he developed early and felt was very important was a commitment to what he somewhat idiosyncratically but suggestively called "visionary" (*hazutit*) language and that he contrasted with metaphor. Visionary language, as he conceived it, was not entirely unmetaphorical but rather resisted being easily broken up into separate figures of speech. As an example of this concept, he juxtaposed two biblical passages, the visions in chapter 6 of Isaiah and the first chapter of Ezekiel. While these passages are similar, Ben-Yosef argued that Isaiah's language could be dismantled into separate units of metaphor, simile, and other figures of speech. Ezekiel's figures of speech, by contrast, seem less daring than plainly descriptive, and form a textual fabric less susceptible to dissection. Ben-Yosef argued that while neither mode is better than the other, the former is more favored by critics, and by poets more popular with critics, since it offered clearly detachable figures of speech, the isolation and analysis of which would "explain" the poem. "Visionary" language does not similarly reduce and so is less amenable to the work of the literary critic.

Formally, Ben-Yosef's poetry is wide-ranging, from free-verse lyrics to formal verse, though he most often favored rhymed and unrhymed iambic pentameter, a rhythm he brought with him from English poetry (though it already existed in Hebrew poetry). The main division in his poetry, however, is not between formal and free verse, or between his conceptions of "visionary" and "metaphorical" language, but between rhymed and unrhymed poems. This division is more than simply formal as it often involves two different stances towards reality. Ben-Yosef's unrhymed poems are more likely to make use of the vocabulary of scientific modernity and more likely to deal with the concrete specificities of the present and recent past. As Ben-Yosef noted, when his unrhymed poems deal with themes of redemption and otherworldliness, they treat these states as things yearned for, not actual. His rhymed poems, by contrast, often seek to instantiate a perfected or redeemed sense of the world in their form, tone, and structure. The shift in his poetry we see from the mid-1980s on toward more overt and frequent treatment of religious themes is therefore accompanied by a greater use of rhyme, to the near total exclusion of free verse. Overall, I find his unrhymed poems, the formal expression of his (and our) lack of redemption, to be more compelling. While Ben-Yosef wrote many riveting poems that employ rhyme schemes, many others, especially the later ones he composed in a more consciously religious or metaphysical mode, display a lack of tension, a balance so perfect as to seem placid, remote. In addition, his affection for his wife sometimes spilled over into sweet, minor poems in rhymed quatrains that read as private ditties rather than as public work. It is for these reasons as much as the greater difficulty of carrying rhyme effectively from one language to another that my selection of Ben-Yosef's poems leans more toward his unrhymed poems than the corpus as a whole reflects.

❧

While Ben-Yosef was first and foremost a poet, he also published a number of short stories, many critical essays about Hebrew poetry and

Jewish nationalism, and two autobiographical novels. Of this output, only the novels achieve independent aesthetic distinction, especially the second. As a critic, Ben-Yosef was sometimes illuminating about the works he discussed (mainly by writers of the pre-state generation) and interesting in his meditations on aesthetics, form, and comparisons between artistic media, but overall his essays are mainly useful as guides to his own ideological and aesthetic preferences. Similarly, his first novel is a fascinating source of biographical information and sensitively drawn vignettes but not entirely successful as a unified work of imaginative fiction. Written in 1971, the novel, titled *Haderekh hazarah* (The Way of Return), covers the story of his and Yehudit's courtship and marriage in Europe, their decision to emigrate to Israel, and the opposition of Ben-Yosef's parents, ending with his and Yehudit's arrival at their new kibbutz home in 1959. Ben-Yosef's portrait of himself at the ages of nineteen and twenty is profound and honest: he is often tyrannical, melodramatic, self-absorbed, a young and temperamental writer, convinced of the worthlessness of his American origins and equally convinced of the Zionist solution to it. He is a romantic, a utopian, who will reinvent himself at any cost, and so reinvent his orphaned wife as well. There are notes of guilt here, as when his alter ego in the novel reflects proleptically on the sacrifices and difficulties demanded of his wife in joining him on their life's adventure. The novel also illustrates the slow flickering into life of his Jewish consciousness, often most interesting when it is portrayed as a matter of pre-conscious affinity (the young protagonist gravitating toward the Jewish heroine of Racine's *Berenice*, for instance, or gazing at Rembrandt's biblical paintings) or the way the Holocaust and Israel hover like ominous but elusive shadows, not yet graspable by the assimilated protagonist. In one extraordinary scene, Ben-Yosef and Yehudit bask in the glow of their young love while watching an anti-Semitic passion play performed in an abbey in York.

The novel is also highly suggestive in its indication of the trajectory Ben-Yosef might have followed had he never arrived at any kind of Jewish national consciousness and stayed in the United States. His lack of interest in America's challenges during the Cold War, despite serving in the U.S. army, and his contempt for his parents' bourgeois existence ready him for the counterculture that would fully emerge there in just another few years. Yet in the late 1950s, his revolutionary muse was not Dean Moriarity or Paul Goodman but his artist friend Barry Fogelson (named Jerry in the novel), who presented aliyah as the best rebellion against the inauthenticity of American life and the anomie of Western culture. As mentioned earlier, this was bound up with an anti-modernist artistic program, a devotion to classicism and the old masters (Racine and Rembrandt are relevant not only for their biblical subject matter), and a conviction that Israel was the place where the artist could find an organic connection to his society.

And this is one of the limitations of the novel: that this dream is presented with neither a convincing indication of its practicability nor the wiser perspective, ironic or mournful, of hindsight. When Ben-Yosef writes that he and Yehudit and Barry "would settle in the land of light and fill it with painting, dance, and poetry" (1973, 115), one isn't sure how to take this—naïvely sincere? retrospectively ironic?—even though by then he had had over a decade to assess the susceptibility of the land of light to being so filled.

Haderekh hazarah is suspended precariously between novel and memoir. The narrative structure is driven by life events and episodes that, while interesting, read like an autobiographical chronicle with a few name changes rather than a work of novelistic imagination. The notable exceptions are the portions told from Yehudit's perspective, obviously something that would be out of place in a memoir, and that may explain Ben-Yosef's impulse to put his story in a form in which Yehudit could be as much the protagonist as himself. One also notes the novel's transmutation of nearly everything (except for names) into a Hebrew stripped of foreign elements, despite the American, British, and German environments and speakers. Ben-Yosef includes several of his own English poems from that period, translated into Hebrew, in the text, and even includes several translated Christmas carols. The novel appears to have answered a need to render his diaspora past entirely in Hebrew. Despite these tensions, and the mixed reviews the novel received, Ben-Yosef was encouraged when in 1975 Doubleday expressed interest in some sample chapters translated into English by him and Yehudit, though no American publisher ever went ahead with publication.

Though just as autobiographical, Ben-Yosef's other novel, *Mirmah* (Deceit), is far more successful. Indeed, from the first line—"It sometimes happens that a man thinks he has been deceived, and later discovers that he had deceived himself" (1979, 5)—the novel projects a feeling of moral weight that recalls the work of the great Israeli writer S. Y. Agnon. Whereas *The Way of Return* is an ideological novel without a clear Archimedean point, and therefore its devotion to biographical detail seems episodic, *Deceit* is a *conte morale*, its personal detail drawn successfully into an aesthetic whole. Or it is altered when necessary: the Ben-Yosef alter ego in the novel has no siblings, and we are told at the start that his parents "who had practically disowned him when he made aliyah many years before, had died together in an airplane crash on their way from New York to Florida. The plane had fallen into the sea and their burial site would never be known" (9).

Written in 1979 and immediately accepted for publication by Amir Gilboa, then editor at Masadah publishing house, *Deceit* is structured around a case of financial fraud to which Ben-Yosef had fallen victim a few years earlier when he invested some money with an acquaintance who absconded with the sum, small but crucial given Ben-Yosef's financial situation, which had markedly deteriorated beginning in the early 1970s. However, this seedy episode is merely the point around which coalesces a novel of protest against what Ben-Yosef saw as the corruption in Israeli society in the years following the Yom Kippur War. He finds the Israelis around him materialistic and Americanizing, purchasing big cars, avoiding military duty, blaring American pop songs from the radio during the Sabbath. The novel is a continuation of his first in the sense that *The Way of Return* explains how he left America while *Deceit* responds to the question of how well or poorly Israel has matched his hopes two decades after immigration. Did Israel deceive him? Did he deceive himself? "He could not escape the thought that perhaps here too some error had been made," he writes in Kafkaesque fashion about his decision to emigrate, "some mistake of his that did in fact constitute a serious crime, a punishment that he had to bear and that even punished his family along with him" (80).

Deceit is of a piece with other Israeli novels of the time—for example, Amos Oz's *The Hill of Evil Counsel* (1976), Yaakov Shabtai's *Past Continuous* (1977), Benjamin Tammuz's *Requiem for Na'aman* (1978)—that similarly pose the question of whether the idealistic promise of the Zionist vision has not somehow been betrayed by the realities of the contemporary state. Ben-Yosef's novel shares the darkness of these others but affirms the truth of the dream by seeking, through a kind of second aliyah, to correct what Ben-Yosef presents as his own self-deception. This second aliyah is both inward—to his family and away from the blandishments of Israeli materialism—and upward, geographically and spiritually, to Jerusalem, where they moved in 1976. The novel expresses the writer's sense of loneliness and isolation, yet also his hopeful new start in Jerusalem and his celebration of the children and wife who give his life its deepest meaning.

∾

As mentioned, Ben-Yosef's finances began to deteriorate in the early 1970s. His mother did not offer support, and it is not likely he would have accepted it if she had. His situation was not helped by the extensive demands of reserve duty—he was promoted to higher rank several times and usually served one to two months a year in a combat unit, time away from both writing and employment. When not on duty, he supported his family through translation—despite his ambivalence about translating into English, which he referred to as a "foreign language"—and through occasional editorial work. This was not especially remunerative, but he stubbornly refused to take nonliterary work or to compromise his literary principles. When he was hired in 1975 as a part-time assistant editor for the literary section of *Maariv*, he quit after a few months since the newspaper was mainly interested in him as a potential cultural conduit for American and English literature; he only wanted to promote Hebrew writers. He began to accumulate debt, and to keep an income he took on more and more translation work, which left less time for his own writing. He sold his possessions to pay bills: the movie camera his parents had given him, his English typewriter, most of his library of English and American poetry.

This was a major reason for his and Yehudit's decision to move to Jerusalem. In order to stabilize their finances, Ben-Yosef and Yehudit decided to sell their home in the Tel Aviv area and find a smaller, less expensive house in which to live. This gave them the opportunity not only to extricate themselves from debt and considerable anxiety, but to fulfill their growing desire to live in the Israeli capital. In 1976, they moved into a little house at the edge of the East Talpiot neighborhood of Jerusalem that abutted the desert and some scattered Arab villages and had a view from their balcony of the Dead Sea. Their third child was born that year.

Money problems never fully disappeared. Yet Ben-Yosef was eventually hired by the education ministry in Jerusalem to teach creative writing and literature, a position that, while by no means lucrative or even secure (he was dismissed in 1992), was the family's bulwark against extreme poverty for more than a decade. His heavy schedule of reserve duty continued into the 1980s, and when Israel invaded Lebanon in 1982, though he had already been on active duty for a month, he was sent to the front and served an additional forty-one days. He was finally released from reserve duty in 1990, having served in three wars and during the Palestinian Intifada (when the windows of his house, being at the edge of Jewish Jerusalem, were repeatedly smashed during the many riots).

∽

"My greatest problem," Ben-Yosef once wrote, "will always be this: that I have no roots in common with any other writer" (1998, 63). He moved to Israel to be a poet with his people, but despite his literary talent and the awards he garnered, he had difficulty finding either a large readership or an enduring literary community.

He hated cliques, schools, movements. He was uninterested in, and sometimes antagonistic to, his most well-known contemporaries, the Israeli poets who began to exert their influence in the 1950s and '60s. It is one of the several ironies of Ben-Yosef's literary career that he rejected not only the United States but also the literary-cultural matrix of Anglo-American modernism at precisely the time that a new generation of Israeli poets—including Yehuda Amichai, David Avidan, and above all Natan Zach—were mining this tradition, seeking models in Anglo-American modernism for a poetics of irony, understatement, private individuality, and colloquial speech as against the heightened rhetoric and collective, vatic quality of much Hebrew poetry in the 1930s and '40s. By contrast, in 1966 Ben-Yosef wrote, "At this time when the direction of Israeli poetry is leading to a decidedly colloquial language, I'm trying to distance myself from this language and to create beauty, not from the easy opposition between poetry and everyday speech, but from a realm specific to poetic utterance" (78). Ben-Yosef found poetic models in early medieval *piyutim* (hymns) and in eighteenth-century Hebrew odes, and felt himself as close to, say, the fourteenth-century Hebrew poet Emanuel of Rome as to the twentieth-century Hebrew poet Natan Alterman.

Nevertheless, Ben-Yosef's poetry does find considerable kinship with his more famous contemporaries, especially with Amichai in the poignant interplay between individual voice and national burden in their military and erotic poems, but also with Zach and Avidan in their formal intricacy and biblical play. What separated him from these poets was more ideological than literary. These writers saw themselves standing on a world stage, not an exclusively Israeli or Jewish one. They cultivated a western-oriented cosmopolitanism that Ben-Yosef sought to exchange for national rootedness. He avoided their predilection for irony as the dominant mode of engagement with the Jewish textual tradition, and though he was not conventionally religious, he was cool toward the absurdist-existentialist and secular humanist outlooks of so many of his contemporaries.

Ben-Yosef was adamantly out of step. He was a passionate Jewish nationalist who believed in a metaphysical and organic concept of Jewish peoplehood: that his people had an intrinsic essence that must be expressed through their culture, society, and politics; that this essence was distorted or harmed when it followed non-Jewish cultural models; and that it was incumbent upon the Hebrew writer to give authentic expression to this essence, not least by drawing from all historical periods of Hebrew literature, not only contemporary Israeli spoken Hebrew and biblical Hebrew but everything in between.

He therefore experienced an increasing sense of cultural and ideological alienation in Israel. Sometimes this took political form, as in his disgust with the country's exhilaration over the peace process with Egypt in the late 1970s. Referring sarcastically to Begin and Sadat as "the messiahs" (1998, 177), he looked upon the notion of making peace with a dictatorial regime that had only a few years earlier launched a brutal war against Israel as a disgusting spectacle that represented Jewish self-deception and Israel's willingness to bow to American pressure. Similarly, he felt that widespread opposition to the invasion of Lebanon in the early 1980s was too often exploited by politicians who sought power by making cynical appeals to hollow moral concerns, echoed by a populace that disregarded its actual, precarious position in the region. He was surprised when he had difficulty publishing his Lebanon war poems. One editor at a prominent press warned him that no Israeli publisher would touch such poems because treating the war in any kind of patriotic light was considered a "sin" (214).

Nevertheless, he never sought a home on the political right, and was as ready to criticize Likud governments as Labor governments. He could not imagine affiliating his poetry with only one political segment of society, and even went so far as to destroy several poems when he felt they were too critical of the Israeli public. In his personal and literary friendships, he never let politics be determinative. His criticisms of Israeli society were less narrowly political than a product of his romantic nationalism. As the literary scholar Nurit Govrin, a friend of Ben-Yosef, has said, he seemed in the 1960s like a man who had stepped out of the Zionism of the 1920s.

Indeed, he gravitated toward older writers, and not even primarily his immediate elders but writers two generations older. The writers whom he admired, befriended, and who took a special interest in his work included Amir Gilboa (born in 1917), Haim Hazaz (born in 1898), Anda Amir-Pinkerfeld (born in 1902), Moshe Shamir (born in 1921), Anadad Eldan (born in 1924), and above all the poet Shin

Shalom (born in 1904), who became a father figure to Ben-Yosef in the course of a friendship that began in the 1970s. These writers, in whom Ben-Yosef recognized the pioneering nationalism and cultural convictions of the pre-state period, constituted Ben-Yosef's first and in many ways most enduring literary community.

A second and in some ways overlapping group of writers to whom Ben-Yosef was drawn were those Hebrew writers who had emigrated from Europe to the United States in the early twentieth century and participated in the development of a little-known but significant Hebrew literary center there. Ben-Yosef admired the literary classicism, Hebrew erudition, and cultural nationalism of these American Hebrew writers, a number of whom, after residing for decades in the United States, moved to Israel after the founding of the state. He went so far as to compare the American Hebrew poets Shimon Halkin, Avraham Regelson, Israel Efros, and Aaron Zeitlin to the giants of medieval Hebrew poetry in Spain.[1] Ben-Yosef visited frequently with Halkin in Jerusalem in the late 1970s; the older writer (Halkin was born in 1898) was enthusiastic about his work. And the institutions of Hebrew culture these writers had helped to develop in the United States were supportive of Ben-Yosef, as were American-residing Hebrew activists and scholars such as Milton Arfa and Haim Leaf. Ben-Yosef won a number of literary honors from American Hebrew institutions, including the Kovner Prize from the Jewish Book Council (twice), and the Neuman Prize for Hebrew literature awarded by New York University. Ben-Yosef received this award in 1979, and was the youngest recipient out of an illustrious group that included Agnon, Hazaz, Lea Goldberg, and Aharon Appelfeld. Most importantly, Ben-Yosef

1. Despite editing a selected poems of the American Hebrew poet Gabriel Preil, Ben-Yosef was discernably less enthusiastic about Preil, who was more of a modernist than a classicist, and who, unlike the other American Hebrew poets mentioned, never cared to move to Israel. For a fuller treatment of the American Hebrew poets, see my *American Hebrew Literature: Writing Jewish National Identity in the United States* (Syracuse UP, 2011) and Alan Mintz's *Sanctuary in the Wilderness* (Stanford UP, 2012).

received several crucial financial subventions from the Metz Fund (set up by the manufacturer of Ex-Lax), the only significant source of funding for Hebrew literature in the United States.

A third group of writers with which Ben-Yosef found fellowship was an odd and occasional quartet consisting of, besides Ben-Yosef himself, the poet Itamar Yaoz-Kest, whose first poems were written during World War II in Bergen-Belsen and who immigrated to Israel in his late teens; Shimon Ballas, a former member of the Israeli Communist Party who had emigrated from Baghdad in the early 1950s and emerged in the 1960s as the major Mizrahi figure in Israeli prose fiction; and Yaakov Beser, a poet who emigrated from the Soviet Union in his teens. In truth, these writers had little in common except for their shared sense of being outsiders to the Israeli literary mainstream, above all because each had grown up without a background in Hebrew and arrived in Israel as teens or adults, after the founding of the state. Together with Ben-Yosef, they published *Mamashut kefulah* (Double Reality), a 1977 anthology of their work, but while their friendships continued they did not continue to publish together.

Ben-Yosef felt that he lacked a genuine readership, though his poetry did achieve minor but not inconsiderable success. When his large volume of selected poems, *Shirim b'olam rotet,* appeared in 1989, for instance, it received not a single review for three months. Yet in time it gave rise to a few positive articles and then a day symposium at Bar-Ilan University, and ended up winning a Keren Hayesod Prize the following year. Most of his books sold out their printings. And yet none of the awards he won could undo his acute sense of isolation or bridge the yawning gap between his original aspirations to be a national poet and the reality of a literary culture that, even if it had use for a national poet, was not inclined to see its image reflected in the particular mirror of Ben-Yosef's poetry.

He therefore looked ahead to a readership that did not yet exist. As early as 1974 he wrote, "There's no sense in striving for acceptance by the Israeli public. I know clearly that my writing will be preserved and will reach its readers over the generations, until those solitary individuals make up a great people like that which I had hoped to be received by here. At this time and place the efforts of someone like me won't succeed, but in the course of time a mighty population will grow that will one day enjoy my lonely efforts" (1998, 142).

◈

What makes Ben-Yosef's story all the more fascinating is that it is a family story. It is a story of oceanic gulfs of sorrow, resentment, and incomprehension across which he and his siblings launched their missives, sometimes of complaint, yet often of love and the desire for reconciliation and closeness. While Ben-Yosef was writing about his American family members, they were writing about him. In the 1970s, Ben-Yosef's younger brother James published the first of several highly praised collections of poems, a few of which deal with their sibling rivalry. In 1986, Ben-Yosef's brother-in-law William Luvaas published a first novel that was clearly inspired by the Reiss family. Ben-Yosef's letters to America are therefore joined by his family members' letters to Israel, through which the Reiss family collectively created its own literature of the American–Israeli relationship in miniature, the conflicts and rifts, rivalries and loyalties of family members and competing homelands.

Two months before Ben-Yosef's "Letters to America" was first published in the 1977 Passover supplement of the newspaper *Maariv*, a poem appeared in the *New York Times* that had won first prize in New York City's bicentennial poetry contest. Far from calling for Jews to move to Israel, this poem celebrated the Jewish experience in the United States. Its title, "New York Is My City," was an implicit rebuttal to the notion that the Jew is only at home in Zion. The speaker declared his fidelity not to biblical patriarchs or Zionist pioneers, but to his immigrant forebears, "sweat-spangled elders / who arrived in this city on ships / in rag shirts and European shoes / and made the sidewalks leap to meet their feet." In America, this other Promised Land, the speaker was

king of the hill
hoisted shoulder-high over 181st Street

by every aproned butcher and candystore man

. . . .

Here where merely to walk down
to the river is an experience
etched in azure. (Reiss 2003, 30)

The poem was written by Ben-Yosef's younger brother, James
Reiss. Reiss is an accomplished poet and a professor (now emeritus) of
English at Miami University in Ohio. His poems are vivid and surpris-
ing, omnivorous in their New York City diction. His first collection,
The Breathers, appeared in 1974 and was reviewed admiringly by crit-
ics such as Helen Vendler in the *New York Times*. One of the poems
in the collection meditated on his father Joseph's death in language
alternately demotic—"Looking at those snapshots of last August, I
see / the emphysema in your eyes, the barrel chest, hump / back, and
pot belly of its final stages" (2003, 9)—and visionary:

The sun went down and the moon blew up.
Then I found my father on the floor
of an ocean of stars like a fish
whose veins were grayer than ash,
whose half-open eyes were covered with silt,
whose split tongue sang like a stone. (11)

It cannot be accidental that Ben-Yosef's first attempt at a poem
entitled "Letter to My Brother"—that is, the germ of his "Letters to
America"—was, according to his diary, undertaken just after James
Reiss's book was published. Most likely, the appearance of his younger
brother's first book provoked Ben-Yosef to treat their common fam-
ily subjects on his own terms and in his own language. As we see in
"Letters to America," Ben-Yosef resented the fact that he could read
his brother's poems but not the reverse. Ben-Yosef describes and iden-
tifies himself with his Hebrew volumes, sent to his brother and that he
imagines are stored unread in a professor's office:

on a shelf by diplomas certifying
a foreign nation's wisdom you've laid your brother

to rest, to gather dust at the feet of idols
in your air-conditioned study, a rare artifact,
a paper mummy preferable to a rotting corpse. (1978, 64)

The resentment cut both ways. Ben-Yosef could be merciless as an older sibling, imperious, angry, stingy of praise. In the younger Reiss's second collection, *Express* (1983), the poem "Brothers" begins,

Eighteen years you beat me over the head
with the butt end of our brotherhood.
So where are you now, Mr. Top
Dog on the Bunk Bed, Mr. Big
Back on the High School Football Team? (Reiss 2003, 26)

"Israel," writes Reiss, was, in the context of their relationship, only another forbidden territory for the younger sibling, "another locked toy / closet on your side of the bedroom, split / by electric train tracks." The poem ends with a bitter toast to his unhappy relationship with his older brother,

whose only gifts to me were kicks

in the teeth, his cast-off comic books,
and worst of all, wrapped, sharpened
for a lifetime,
the perfect razor of my rage.

Yet in the same collection, Reiss also meditates with honest clarity upon the family dynamic in which Cecilia's too-intense love for Ben-Yosef cost the elder brother his father's affection. The title poem in *Express* is a triptych of imagined monologues by James, his father, and Ben-Yosef, in which the father posthumously admits, "how I bloomed for you, my second son— / I was a spiny cactus for your brother" (2003, 37), associating the Israeli desert of Ben-Yosef's current locale with the absence of fatherly love in his childhood. The father continues: "Him I adored until his mother's kiss / found me jealous, hateful," while the monologue Reiss imagines his older brother delivering recalls their father's brutal silences and foul moods, and ends,

Now I quicken in a duplex with a view
of the Arab Quarter: My window overlooks
a stretch of desert tenanted by Moslems.
I shop in bazaars where veiled women scorn cameras,
selling hummus and falafel to my wife and children.
I stare west between the Suez Canal
and Italy's boot—seven thousand miles—until
I conjure your face, sky-blue in rigor mortis,
and kiss the frozen shutters of your eyelids. (38)

Beginning in the 1980s and especially after Cecilia's death in 1999, there was a slow rapprochement between the siblings, finally out of their parents' shadow if not of the memory of old wounds. In his 1996 collection *The Parable of Fire*, Reiss's poem "Ammunition Hill" describes this wariness, in which the Jerusalem locale of a bloody battle in the Six Day War becomes symbolic of the two brothers' conflictual past and continuing ability to register and inflict pain. "Can brothers set aside the holy wars / they waged as children?" he asks, describing Ben-Yosef and himself as "Cain and Abel in the fields / their parents planted out of ignorance" (2003, 69). We recall that Ben-Yosef's first collection, in English, contained the poem "Cain and Abel," which described two "brothers stuffed with murder and curse" (Ben-Yosef 1959, 17). "Ammunition Hill" concludes, "My brother wanders past a captured tank / on blocks, picks up a stone, and turns to me" (Reiss 2003, 69). These tense lines resonate with that first biblical murder of younger brother by older. Even more audaciously, Reiss's image links Ben-Yosef with the media images of Palestinian rioters in the First Intifada.

~

A 1960s bildungsroman and elegy for the American counterculture, *The Seductions of Natalie Bach* is throbbingly lyrical, erotic, and often breathtaking in the extent of the author's imaginative habitation of his characters. Published in 1986, it was the debut novel of William Luvaas. Given that Luvaas was raised in a Lutheran family in Oregon, it is notable that in this novel he chose not to portray the Pacific Northwest but rather New York City and a collection of passionately conflicted Jewish characters. These include the eponymous heroine of the novel, an artist rebelling against the expectations of her bourgeois parents, and her older brother, whose parallel rebellion against their parents consists of his decision to move to Israel. Luvaas's choice of subject matter becomes less unexpected when we learn that his wife is the artist Lucinda Luvaas, the younger sister of Ben-Yosef. The fictional character of Natalie is clearly based on Lucinda, and Natalie's Zionist older brother Adam is just as clearly based on Luvaas's brother-in-law Ben-Yosef. One would not want to take the point too far: *The Seductions* is a work of fiction, not documentary, and Natalie and Adam, despite their inspiration, are hardly identical with Lucinda and Robert Reiss. Yet Luvaas's novel constitutes, like the poetry of James Reiss, another instance in which, while Ben-Yosef was writing his letters to America, his American family members were writing their own letters back. Not that Ben-Yosef ever read the novel that so clearly draws on his own dramas and those of the Reiss family. Nor were Luvaas or Ben-Yosef's sister Lucinda able to read the "Mikhtavim la'Ameriqah" until its recent translation. These "letters" were all unread, yet powerfully felt. It seems clairvoyant when, in the novel, Natalie writes in a letter to a friend, "I don't really even expect you to answer this letter. I'm not that naïve anymore. And letters are satisfying by themselves. First you write them, then you read them. So, in a way, they answer themselves" (Luvaas 1986, 217).

While Natalie is the novel's protagonist, she is somewhat dwarfed by two other characters, a man and a woman who offer models for the freedom and authenticity she seeks. The first of these is her older brother, Adam. A jazz pianist and college dropout, Adam has found his road to self-creation and freedom by moving with his wife to Israel and joining a kibbutz near the Syrian border, to the dismay of his wealthy parents and the fascinated ambivalence of his sister. "There are two ways to live," he tells his sister. "You can be a drone, obedient to what's expected of you, or you can take life in hand like clay and make what you want of it" (124).

"Adam's philosophy," Natalie reports, "is that one has to abandon the past completely and find life on his own. Each one of us has to be Adam/Eve all over again, not just wimpily accept our fate and ape our parents' ways" (217–18). And Natalie joins her older brother in Israel for a time—just as Lucinda spent time at Kibbutz Cabri with Ben-Yosef and Yehudit. But in both cases, the younger sister would not adopt the older brother's Zionism as the basis for her own rebellion and search for artistic autonomy. In the novel, Natalie challenges Adam:

> Once, feeling brave, I said that according to his philosophy his own children must rebel some day. Maybe even abandon Israel. The Pentateuch Patriarch looked at me like I'm loony. "Nonsense," he said, "Israel is the only secure and sensible place for a Jew to live. It has nothing to do with me. Nothing at all." (217–18)

Natalie continues explaining her rejection of Adam's path, likening his Jewish nationalism to the American jingoism she detests:

> So maybe Ma/Pa Bach made a mistake and maybe it's some wonderful dream to be part of something bigger—a People, a Nation— that I'm missing out on in life. But I'm not sure I believe it. Not even sure there's any difference between puffing out your chest and squawking "I'm Jewish, I'm Jewish!" and potting out your belly, wearing a flag lapel button and fat American smile and shouting, "I'm American thru and thru and I hate all the rest of you." (218)

Nevertheless, she admires Adam's impulse if not the form it takes. "Maybe in a way I am like Adam," she reflects, "looking for some better solution to life" (219). And while she may reject his ideology and overbearing persona, Adam's integrity inspires Natalie throughout, and his outsized presence haunts most every part of the novel.

The other model of authenticity offered to Natalie is the character of Maxine Pearlman. Maxine is the novel's triumph, an irresistibly attractive character one can't help but fall in love with: she is charismatic, ebullient, honest, sensual, life-affirming. Maxine, who begins the novel as Natalie's teacher and nearly becomes her lover, is proudly Jewish in the New York, socialist, Yiddishkeit mode. She is the American

Jewish path in contrast to Adam's Zionist Israeli path, yet is presented as a kind of twin or complement to him rather than an antagonist. In fact, when Adam and Maxine meet, they flirt with each other and it is strongly implied that they have an affair (one of many reminders that Luvaas is engaged in fiction, not biography). Maxine teases Natalie for her assimilated upbringing, albeit without Adam's rigid disdain. And she recognizes that Adam is pursuing a parallel track to her own, seeing his Zionism as another form of countercultural transformation. "We can liberate ourselves," she tells Natalie at one point. "Beyond the big issues there's social progress on a personal level, becoming what we believe is right. Like your brother Adam" (124).

Ultimately, Natalie pursues her own idiosyncratic path in the United States, where the messianic stirrings of the American counterculture seem to her like "an Israel around us" (131). She does not follow Adam's nationalist vision, nor Maxine's keen social conscience, nor even the option proffered by Gene—the stand-in for Luvaas himself—a quiet man she meets in the redwood forests of California and who aches to have children with her, something Natalie rejects in order to devote herself wholly to painting and sculpture. (This is in striking contrast to Ben-Yosef's "Letters to America," in which his sister's childlessness is portrayed as somehow linked to her husband's Christian provenance.) At the end of the book, Natalie comes to the conclusion that for her there is no Promised Land anywhere, only a permanent and quite wonderful exile. "Artists are nomadic, like the Jews," she says, in implicit opposition to her older brother's nationalist vision of Jewishness and art alike. "Diaspora isn't any temporary dislocation; it's our understanding of things" (326).

The distance between Luvaas's fictional Adam and the real Ben-Yosef is most evident in the novel's presentation of Adam's decision to emigrate. Rather than Ben-Yosef's beliefs in Jewish national belonging and authenticity, Adam is driven by a morbid obsession with the Holocaust and anti-Semitism, something that did not afflict Ben-Yosef. Luvaas transmutes Barry Fogelson into an improbable ultra-orthodox American Jewish soldier named Pavel whom Adam meets while stationed in Germany. "In snapshots, Pavel always to the side, hollow-cheeked and sickly, with sallow, translucent skin and liquid Kafkaish eyes, an inward Orthodox air about him. Earlocks and yarmulke seeming antithetical to his uniform" (62). Rather than discussing the possibilities for art and poetry on the kibbutz as Barry Fogelson did, Pavel takes Adam on a tour of the concentration camps in Europe. When Natalie visits Adam in New York soon afterwards, she finds that, in his apartment, "everywhere, mixed amongst Hebrew and Jewish history texts, were periodicals with alarmist headlines proclaiming rising anti-Semitism in America. . . . I often left that apartment with a creepy feeling that I wasn't in America at all, but prewar Poland, barely resisting an urge to feel my sleeve for a yellow Star of David" (61).

Similarly, Luvaas's Israel is not Ben-Yosef's Israel, a place of hope for Jewish national renaissance that is simultaneously undermined by assimilation and Americanization. The Israel we encounter in *The Seductions* is a place of thuggishness and a rather different kind of failure, the moral degeneration of the Jews through their treatment of the Arabs. The writing of both Luvaas and James Reiss reflect a wariness about Jewish nationhood, which is sometimes seen as existing necessarily at the expense of a suffering Palestinian population. Adam reports in an early letter, "I come in dismay upon a roadblock where Jewish soldiers stop and search Arab cars, insulting occupants and shoving them about with rifle butts. Once (I hesitate to write this to my sister) I saw a Jewish soldier pull a Palestinian woman from a car by her skirt, raising it to the amusement of his buddies. I ran over, shouting, 'We aren't Nazis'" (64). The modern Jewish national project, the intricacies of Israeli and Jewish history, the cultural stakes of Hebrew, are replaced in the novel by the binaristic portrayal of the Jews as either morally pristine, piously earlocked and powerless, or callous soldiers becoming the new Nazis. In keeping with this typology, Adam is unable to learn Hebrew and so despondent over the failures of Israel that he is on the verge of suicide until a supernatural episode in which an old Hasidic Jew in caftan and shtreimel charges him to live, and to defend Israel but "never to persecute. You have seen how our soldiers abuse the law. Our righteousness is as a filthy rag. Wisdom is greater than strength, ben Yaakov. Never forget" (65). The Hasid vanishes and Adam realizes that their entire conversation has been in Hebrew, acquired magically.

✧

From his first books to his last, the most constant subject of Ben-Yosef's poetry is his relationship with his wife Yehudit. His feelings for his wife produced many of his finest poems, which roil with erotic intensities and explore marital passion, sex, and aging with stunning force and beauty. The sight of his wife's body, dancing or sleeping, was for Ben-Yosef as perpetually miraculous as his own astonished and grateful presence in the holy land.

Often, his poems about Yehudit are voyeuristic episodes in which he watches her, photographs her, films her, observes her looking at herself in the mirror. We find him again and again in his early books studying her sleeping form, when she appears as conquered or dead, yet perfect and inaccessible and even threatening to him in her still, marmoreal perfection. While she is presented as pure and clean, he is dirty, polluting, disarmed by his perpetual need for her and inability to possess her as fully as he would like. In the poem "Badimdumim" (At Twilight), he is a melancholy supplicant at Yehudit's bedside:

> you are sleeping, I won't wake you
> even though my head bends thirsty to you, I won't muddy with my
>   kiss
> the clarity of your cheek or ripple of your lips as they breathe,
> won't rouse you from your perfection lest the arid cracks
> of hope pass from my brow to mar the crown in you. (1969, 44)

Sex, that "demand for mercy" (44), is, as in his "Lion" poems, a conquest that conquers the conqueror. The predator is ever undone by his prey. The sharp edges of these jealousies and vulnerabilities are worn away over time, in a poetic record of a marital passion that never cools but is nevertheless tempered by parenthood, age, and experience. In the extraordinary "Poem of Grafts," Ben-Yosef "grafts" erotic memories of a vacation with his wife in the Sinai peninsula in 1972 together with components of Israeli national history and memory such as the Holocaust, the Yom Kippur War, and the Exodus from Egypt:

> at the touch of her body I knew
> that my life has meaning, that I have a world,
> that I have a woman with whom I lie
> passing my hand over her treasures
> abundant like silent coral in the depths
> of memory, and surely I already knew
> there on the shore of the Red Sea
> that I was finally a free man. (1989, 293–94)

He does not conflate them but braids together the national and the personal, the tragic and the romantic.

⤚⧽

The first time I speak with Yehudit is by telephone from the United States. I am calling to interview her about her husband, and I begin by asking her to tell me the story of how they met. "Well," she says softly in an English that is lightly accented with something no longer American yet not quite Israeli either, "it was at Oberlin College, in 1954. And it was just after. . . ." She pauses, groping for a forgotten word, then asks, "What was the holiday you just had?" I hesitate, then offer tentatively, "Thanksgiving?" "Yes, that's it," this daughter of Midwestern Quakers says, "Thanksgiving."

She is a gracious hostess when we meet in her home in the East Talpiot neighborhood of Jerusalem. My three small children are in tow, and so we first spend time at a nearby playground talking while the kids play. Her femininity remains, but in her mid-seventies she is no longer the lithe dancer with the long blonde braid in family photographs. Rather, she resembles a veteran kibbutznikit, a pioneer woman with strong hands and eyes of bright blue. At the house, she sets the table with a satisfying Israeli lunch. The house is small and simply furnished, at least by American standards. The main space is a sitting and dining room that looks out onto the balcony, with a third of the space sectioned off by a set of bookcases whose blank backs face the common area. From the balcony, the Judean desert recedes into its impossible colors.

I ask about Ben-Yosef's religious practice, since his poetry is in some ways deeply religious, or at least decidedly suffused with a conviction of the relationship between the Jewish people, its land, and its God, yet never normative or orthodox. Yehudit explains that they spent their first decade in Israel on secular kibbutzim where there was little in the way of traditional religious observance, and so after leaving the kibbutzim and moving to Tel Aviv her husband began to develop his own Jewish customs, for himself and his family, and was punctilious about observing them even as they changed over time. Theirs was a melange of the secular and the religious. On Friday nights, his family ate together and he led his children in a discussion of the weekly Torah reading. He also taught his children the special "Rashi script" font used in traditional scriptural commentaries, a rare skill among secular Israelis, and he introduced them to the classical commentators. He would smoke on the Sabbath. Saturday mornings he did not go to synagogue but read Psalms and went with his family on a hike, his Sabbath worship directed in classical Zionist fashion toward the land of Israel and the poetry of its people.

Holidays were similar combinations of secular Israel custom, pre-rabbinic observances, and personal creation. For instance, during the eight days of Sukkot, Ben-Yosef and his children would each recite a Hebrew poem a day as a family ritual, usually one of the poems being his own and the others drawn from admired modern and medieval verse. Prior to Passover, the family would go on a camping trip in the desert to feel something of the wandering of the Israelites. On the three biblical pilgrimage festivals—Passover, Sukkot, and Shavuot—he would walk with his children at night to visit the Western Wall, though he did not pray there or even put a written prayer in one of the cracks. The Day of Atonement was usually the occasion for a family camping and hiking trip; he did not begin to fast on the holiday until late in life. Even then, he did not go to synagogue but would spend the day reading aloud one of the books of the Bible.

My children play on the rug beneath a quartet of watercolors by Barry Fogelson, two nudes and two landscapes that all glow with terra-cotta tones and Mediterranean light. I go to the other side of the bookshelves, where Ben-Yosef's weathered writing desk of dark wood has been kept neatly by Yehudit with a not terribly flattering photograph of Ben-Yosef in the center. The narrow window above the desk is lined with potted succulents and offers a view of the limestone wall of the next house over. The shelves house a good Hebrew library, both classical and eclectic as one would expect Ben-Yosef's to be. I notice a Ben-Yehuda dictionary, Herzl's diaries, the Zohar, the Vilna Gaon's commentary on the Book of Esther, histories of the Holocaust and of ancient Israel, and of course dozens of modern Hebrew writers, Ben-Yosef's friends, models, and rivals: Shin Shalom and Moshe Shamir, Uri Zvi Greenberg and Yosef Hayim Brenner, Shaul Tchernikhovsky and Haim Hazaz. On one small set of shelves, I find the remnants of a once large collection of English literature, now reduced to a few dozen survivors: Blake, Spenser, Shakespeare, Matthew Arnold, Dylan Thomas, Langston Hughes, E. E. Cummings, Robinson Jeffers.

ଏ

Tirzah and I meet in a noisy café in the shopping mall in a Jerusalem suburb where the bookstore she manages is located. She takes after her mother's side of the family, with the sturdiness, blonde hair, and smiling blue eyes that make me think of an American farmer's wife. She is married to a financial analyst of Iraqi and Polish descent whom she met during her army service in the intelligence division, and they have a son, then doing his army service, who I learn has inherited his grandfather's musical gifts.

Tirzah's English is accented but excellent. I ask her if she has spent time in the States. Yes, she has visited there three times. The first time was when she was a baby, the visit in 1962 that provided the basis for Ben-Yosef's long poem "The City." The second time, when she was a girl, she and her younger brother Carmi accompanied her parents to Florida when her grandfather Joseph was dying. As Ben-Yosef recounted in the "Letters to America," they arrived the night he died. Soon after the funeral at sea, Tirzah remembers, Ben-Yosef's mother Cecilia started an explosive fight, and Ben-Yosef ended by leaving his parents' house with Yehudit and their children, traveling by Greyhound bus to stay with Yehudit's sister in the northeast. Ben-Yosef had no return tickets to Israel or money, so he worked briefly for the Hebrew activist Milton Arfa to earn money for the return trip. The third time, Tirzah and husband visited the States without her parents. Together with Cecilia, Lucinda and William Luvaas, and James Reiss, they rented a house in upstate New York, a family reunion that helped stitch together these disparate tribes.

The oldest of Ben-Yosef's three children, Tirzah is the only one who remembers her early childhood on the kibbutz, which she did not especially like—she found it upsetting to have to sleep not in a house with her parents but rather in the communal children's quarters. Yet her memories of childhood are overall very happy, and she describes her father as attentive and devoted to his children. She explains that each of the names of Ben-Yosef's children—Tirzah, Carmi, and Naim—can be found in the Song of Songs, and that Ben-Yosef made a song of the verses with their names in it and sang it to them as a bedtime lullaby. She recalls her parents as very social, always entertaining their friends. Her father's friends were either fellow writers—she mentions Anda Amir as being like a grandmother to her—or fellow soldiers. Her traumatic experience, like her father's, was the Yom Kippur War—she tells me the story of how they experienced the outbreak of the war while camping near Mount Meron, with nearby explosions and plumes of smoke announcing the onset of that near-catastrophe. Her coping mechanism in the days that followed was to keep a scrapbook of all the newspaper announcements about her friends' and classmates' fathers and brothers who had been killed or were missing in action, her attempt to conjure for herself at the age of eleven some kind of control while her father was away at the front.

I ask her how her father influenced her. "He was hard," she says, "the way he expected you to be true to yourself." He insisted, "Don't do something that you don't believe in just because that's what other people or the society wants you to do. He was very clear on that, that I should feel in my own conscience what is right and wrong and stand by it. And that made me strong . . . If something is wrong, I won't do it even if everyone else thinks it is okay." She tells me about an incident when she was around ten years old. She liked to draw. "At first I wasn't very good," she says, "so one time I took a picture and I copied it and I showed it to him. And he told me that he didn't like that picture. 'This is copying,' he said. 'Never copy. Do it yourself.' And I did learn to do it myself."

✍

The bus winds through northern Jerusalem, then leaves the city and enters the West Bank through the Hizma Checkpoint. After an hour driving through the rippling, sun-soaked hills, we arrive first at the town of Shiloh, which is named for the biblical city whose ruins are nearby, and then at Eli, named for the biblical priest, a town of 3,000 people who are referred to in the international press as "settlers." This is where I alight. The place is clean and attractive, with quiet pine-shaded streets. Carmi Ben-Yosef meets me and walks me to his home.

Carmi is slender with serious dark eyes, and reminds me of a photograph of his grandfather Joseph. He wears a knitted kippah and tzitzit and sports a beard. He and his wife, a vivacious woman from a Bukharan Jewish family, have six children. We sit in their sunny living room and talk—in Hebrew, since his English is limited—about his father. Carmi was at his father's bedside when he died in 2001 at the age of sixty-three. Ben-Yosef was diagnosed with cancer in 1999, and the disease proved inoperable. With a knack for binding his life to the Jewish calendar, Ben-Yosef had arrived in Israel on the eve of the Jewish New Year, and he passed away on the festival of Purim. At his father's request, Carmi, visiting him in the hospital, read aloud the biblical Scroll of Esther as is customary on the holiday. Several hours afterward, Ben-Yosef died.

I ask Carmi about his own religious observance, since he is the only one of his siblings who is orthodox, let alone who lives in the territories. He explains that he gradually began adopting orthodox religious observance during his army service. I ask how his father reacted to the change, and he responds that he feels his religious observance was a natural extension of his father's own search for the truth. "I followed his path," he says, "but farther."

❧

Naim, the youngest of Ben-Yosef's three children, has both his father's looks—he is tall and broad-shouldered with reddish blonde hair—and the same deep, granite-like voice I have heard in sound recordings of his father reading poetry. Naim's pretty Bulgarian fiancée disappears into a back room while we sit and talk (in a combination of English and Hebrew) at the dining room table in his mother's home. He describes his father as a collection of contradictions. "You could never predict how he would react to something," Naim says. He was easy to anger and easily pacified. He was very rigid about personal loyalty and behavior—he insisted that his children always tell the truth—but he also was entirely nonjudgmental about his children's choices in life. He could be very right wing in his political views, but he never let politics affect his friendships and never exhibited the slightest anti-Arab prejudice.

When I ask about Naim's relationship to the United States, he tells me he has no interest in it. In fact, he prefers Europe to both the United States and Israel. Southern Europe—Italy, France, Greece—is where he feels most at home, drawn to the relaxed Mediterranean lifestyle. I ask about the Jewish observances practiced by his father, and he says that he liked them when he was growing up, and that they still comprise the only part of Jewish tradition he feels a connection to, though over time he has grown distant from them. "Sitting in a European cathedral," he informs me, "is where I find spirituality."

❧

In the 1990s, not long before he died, Ben-Yosef mused that he might yet see the emergence of two potential audiences for his poetry. One was that of the modern religious population in Israel (as opposed to both the secular majority and the ultra-orthodox), who might be expected to appreciate the deep currents of Jewish spirituality and high degree of Jewish literacy in his poetry. And in fact during the 1980s and '90s he found his poetry the object of enthusiastic interest on the part of several talented younger religious and neo-mystical poets such as Rivka Miryam, Elhanan Nir, Shira Twersky-Cassel, and Oded Mizrahi.

The second potential audience he speculated upon in his diary was American Jews. This is surprising given his rejection of the United States, his conviction of the moribund state of American Judaism, and his decided ambivalence about seeing his own work translated into English. As he wrote in a 1974 essay,

> I've never seen myself as belonging to the American Jewish community. Certainly, I was born in New York to Jewish parents, but they sought to sever their connection to the tradition, to erase their past and to be ensconced at any price in the land of unlimited opportunity. And as happens in such cases, the family was left with no unifying bond, was scattered and cut off from its people. . . . When the miracle occurred and it was revealed to me that indeed I was a Jew, I burned all bridges and immigrated as if from a distant exile across the Sambatiyon [a mythical river in Jewish folklore], a place not worth remembering. (1995, 203)

Yet, two decades later, he reflected that, given the particularities of his own biography, it might prove to be the case that some of his future readers would, like him, come from the United States. As he realized, his own life was testimony to the real possibility of the most improbable Jewish renaissances. And in fact, in the essay quoted from above, Ben-Yosef swerves, just after the passage cited, back across the Sambatiyon of his American origins, affirming with surprising and elegantly dialectical irony and hope,

> It is a great privilege to be an assimilated Jew in America today. For it is precisely that assimilated Jew, hardly conscious of his Jewish

heritage, who is in the position to decide for himself. He can choose to be chosen. He can turn blind fate into a source of light. (204)

Portland, Oregon
2014

References

Ben-Yosef, Reuven [as Robert Reiss]. 1959. *The Endless Seed*. New York: Exposition Press.

———. 1965. *Waiting Gulls* [*Shehafim mamtinim*]. Tel Aviv: Hakibutz Hame'uhad.

———. 1967. *The Way of the Land* [*Derekh erets*]. Ramat Gan: Hakibutz Hame'uhad.

———. 1969. *As You Get Dressed* [*Ka'asher at mitlabeshet*]. Tel Aviv: Eqed.

———. 1973. *The Way Back* [*Haderekh hazarah*]. Merhavyah: Sifriyat po'alim.

———. 1974. *The Dead and the Loving* [*Metim ve'ohavim*]. Ramat Gan: Masadah.

———. 1978. *Noon in Jerusalem* [*Tsohorayim biYirushalayim*]. Jerusalem: Agudat Shalem.

———. 1979. *Deceit* [*Mirmah*]. Givatayim: Masadah.

———. 1989. *Selected Poems, 1962–1989* [*Shirim b'olam rotet*]. Tel Aviv: Dvir.

———. 1995. *Essays* [*Al tarbutenu hamitgabeshet*]. Jerusalem: Bitsaron.

———. 1998. *A Writer's Diary* [*Yoman ketivah*]. Jerusalem: Yitakhen.

Luvaas, William. 1986. *The Seductions of Natalie Bach*. Boston: Little, Brown.

Reiss, James. 2003. *Riff on Six: New and Selected Poems*. Cambridge: Salt.

Poems Translated from Hebrew

Waiting Gulls, 1965

❦

3.
As the snow fell, we entered the house prepared for us,
the stove was lit, the table laid with silver and gold,
flowers on the walls, bed spread white, and I wandered
between its white and yours as in a room of mirrors:

the light wavered, the heat went from me, we embraced
to the beat of the snowfall's patter, I exalted you in dance,
by the sparkle of ice on the window I interpreted for you
the symbols of my eyes, until the flowers and the fire went out,

until your eyes darkened like ash. From your flesh I awoke,
and stood listening: not to your breathing, nor to the sound of the
    snow
but to something like the sound of breathing or snow,
whispering from dark corners, surrounding the place where you
    sleep.

Notes to the Poem

This sequence is about Ben-Yosef's early courtship of his wife. The title, "*Kishnei prahim batsiah*," is a phrase from Haim Nahman Bialik's poem "*Im dimdumei hehamah*" (At Twilight). Bialik's poem is not a cheerful love poem but rather describes the sorrow of two lovers whose dream is not attained. Bialik's poem ends (in Robert Friend's translation):

And we have been abandoned
on those islands,

with no companions, no friends—
two flowers of the wilderness,
two lost seeking a world lost
without end, without end.

> *Found in Translation: Modern Hebrew Poets* (New Milford,
> CT: Toby Press, 2006)

The third poem in Ben-Yosef's sequence, translated here, resembles a description in his autobiographical novel *Haderekh hazarah* of a night he and his wife spent in Germany after they were married there. As mentioned in the introduction, there are echoes of Hart Crane's poem "My Grandmother's Love Letters."

In the Room Where I Studied

In the room where I studied, no daylight shone.
Behind drawn curtains, darkness spread
across the skies of Hebrew letters
and my poor, reeling head.

A shack in a stand of pines, by day
the sun drew up bright sparks of green,
though I heard nothing of their ascent
as I toiled behind my screen.

Each night the pines mourned the death of day
Till they slept, exhausted by their laments.
And I wandered on while gloom overtook
the pages' radiance.

Till an unexpected hour came,
and even I was eased, in the way
a tree is eased when it wakes at dawn
and quietly waits for day.

Notes to the Poem

This poem recalls Emily Dickinson in rhythm and form; see the introduction for additional comments. I am indebted in my effort to translate this to Esther Cameron's version.

The Carcass

Far from all human dwellings, on a plain
of sand hammered by the sun, I found the bones,
gleaming smooth and white, uncracked and still

keeping the body's pattern: sharp paws digging
the sand in a silent ceaseless motion,
the head rounding its depression, the neck aligned,

and through the gaps in the ribs, I caught the glint
of golden droplets, shining like the shards
of precious vessels on ruined walls,

and I put forth my hand, and the gold stuck
to my hand, to my cheek, and into my veins
a sweetness descended as I knelt there, tasting

insatiably, the white sand's glare in my eyes,
the sun above me, far from all human dwellings.

Notes to the Poem

Translated by Esther Cameron. The poem references the Samson
story in Judges 14.

From **The City**

1.
After the sea, above water shrinking to the horizon,
in bridges of light after light you appear,
like the revelation after years of those bejeweled arms
crossed over your black lap. My plane descends and circles
above the waves, above electricity, above the hair
covered in brick.

A lovely woman with closed eyes,
a desired woman, her head turned away unresponding,
the sea rolling unceasingly and I returning,
descending over concrete, over glass,
over the leaves etched with spokes of light,
metallic evergreens.

Nights of mighty walls,
the door open to the shore, with no voice calling after me.
I went away, now too there is no sound
except that of the jet engines, my strength bound as I approach
the towers, the chimneys,
the bridges moving in the stream.

The plane passes the last of the roofs,
in the space before contact an old melody is heard,
perhaps the one above your head,
turned away beneath the pressure of shadows,
an old tune rising, rolling like smoke
returning to silence and clarity.

2.
Raindrops leap upon the asphalt,
yellow stains on the windowpanes, below shafts
of light refract: in the dark, endless streets
you loosed your hair.
Puddles extending in the gloom,
flash of a weary smile.

I heard a laugh from one of the doorways in the fog,
clinking of glasses and shining, tinkling bracelets,
my moist breathing hung upon splayed fingers,
not yours, not you;
dark, endless streets,
here as a boy I walked among black veils.

The tune stretches out like a blue snake,
silken arms draw it, twining
among jars of roses and bowls of soggy grain.
A taxi shines a moment at the window,
and my palms yearn for soft, yellow hair.
In the distance tired lips close.

Dark, endless streets,
raindrops leap upon the asphalt, upon my feet,
rising and falling, rising and falling, and I do not gather them,
refugees.
A drunk lies on the sidewalk, I lean over him,
we sway the two of us to the rhythm of the gutters' sough.

3.
My mother through the long dim vestibule
blows me a kiss: many years,
she says, many; the walls enclose her figure
with the dust of old porcelain.
Only her shadow in a room of wide light
waits in the distance.

"Are you listening to me?" I call, my feet
heavy upon the warm carpet.
On the wall are shelves, leather and wood mummies,
here my ivory elephant, and a glass horse,
at the end of the hallway the trembling shadows of hands
on fragments of light.

Many years,
the rage swells up before me like dirt upon a grave,
my mother was here planting her flowerpots,
and I on the sidewalk, on the streaming steel I ran,
I sought,
and in my ears the echoes of my name from the closed windows
    above.

Here, by the shelves, a photograph of me less twenty years,
teeth so brilliant,
here was my mother watering cactuses,
African gladioli, tulips from China.
"Are you listening to me? Are you?"
Between the black walls, the shadow turns gold like a candle.

6.

In sound and fury, flesh enters stone,
cool walls around the car
like thighs leading one's consenting hand in silence,
a secret tunnel,
I came back to your old route, cover me
so I never get out.

A train underneath highway and river,
as a boy I stayed here rocking,
to no station: the passengers
continually being born and dying, and my birth carried on
among the familiar walls, always
new in the dark.

Only here without sun and air did I live,
steel wheels screeching, the rails
driving rhythmically, the tunnel opening
to pull down my light from blackness to blackness.
By the front window I stood,
weak and burning.

Again I come to the window, to seize
the imaginary notion, but a boy stands there,
taking my spot, his fingers spread
against the dark sheet,
against the tunnel suddenly brightening around me, shining
to the point of blindness.

7.
Only the buildings, brick upon brick,
amid the rushing back and forth of color, stand still.
Gray the stones cling to the sky.
A girl enters, fake-fruit hat dripping over her smile,
an old man in a suit of sand.
In a doorway they become one, disappear.

The infants go out in a herd of wheels,
nannies white as a letter, a well-heeled man,
running to a car, takes off flying.
Scrap paper dizzy in the foreground,
and erect shadows, and downcast shadows.
My eyes scatter on the stone like streetlights in the fog.

Ringing intensifies and falls, a blushing siren,
braking trucks gleam like fire,
whistles, axes, hose,
skipping helmets, "they say a boiler
or a stove, to smithereens," in a doorway they become one,
disappear.

Only the buildings, brick upon brick,
the crowd swaying in its hues,
metal, rubies, "they say she was hit in the neck,
tore the veins," stand still in the gloom,
the buildings, my eyes return from them
like a lifeboat from the sea.

10.
My father listened above his reflection in the table
as I listen today above the water, as evening approaches
the piers, the cranes, cables, drums,
silent all, with only a ripple and twilight
moving near,
to the distant call of the shore.

He placed his pencils in the box, the papers
each in their proper file, metal drawers clicked shut,
and the deep sound gaped wide again,
a vision of breakers and foam, from his window my father looked out
on the emptying stores, the people hurrying home,
listened from the high wall.

The tone deepened, yearning, the stores
each in their proper pocket, inhaling his expensive tobacco
my father listened to the rustle of leaves on sand
under the palms, beyond
the electrified streets, the sparkling reflection
in the briefcases and safeboxes.

I look at the pier, at the thousands of waves
striking it, the sharp crane
nailed in the fog, I listen
as my father listened above his table
suspended in the night
to the distant call of our flesh.

11.

Your face I sought to abandon, through the railing your neck
extends a caress, your breasts closed behind flowerpots,
your thighs scrolls of silk I sought to abandon,
your eyes brass candlesticks,
the cup of my drunkenness before the candle, as I return
to the party of shadows.

You move away from the neon signs, from the last streetlamp,
over the tower of glass panes your hair cascades, explodes,
from my muscles fire, from my lips fire, again you distance yourself
    in the siren
echoing across the roofs, there the woman giving birth clenches,
    screams,
network of flesh floating above tears—I
gathered my small day and died.

Your smile in the glass door opening to a door, door to door,
a hall of doorways I sought to abandon,
an empty room only your perfumes, no exit,
creaking of heavy hinges, shock of iron, I land
on the cage floor of your scent, violent shadows upon me,
choking with sweetness.

Your face that of a girl sitting on stairs, a maiden
wrapped in sleeves, a woman with six babies in her skirts,
a longing I sought to end
or abandon beneath the last streetlight, wondering
as I sailed over distant waves,
as my breath flew towards dawn.

12.
The airplane waits for me, and from its windows
flee shadows, the ones I saw
in the streets, in the halls, moving
with the turning gears that rotate
in a blind skeleton.
Over my heart, I heard their oily sound.

My heart that always falls into your lap,
a stone in the dream of failing wells
I go out from among the bricks, only
eyes and memory.
I will create a heart of flesh on the flight,
I will seal your praise in the rock of stars.

The plane waits, flowering hills
wait for me, the crowd of your admirers dispersed,
wandering under streetlamps, and I on quivering asphalt
spread my hands as to one who departs.
My only one I loved you, the others
fell like chips from the statue of a pagan goddess.

You did not come near, you did not respond, you did not listen
to the scrape of my nails on the walls, I go up to the plane,
in bridges of light after light you are extinguished.
I'm already awake, will I hear your name again?
In the gossip of leaves,
or in a star's lullaby.

Notes to the Poem

Crane's "The Bridge" and Eliot's *The Waste Land* are models for a
city of alienation and sorrow. See the introduction for further discus-
sion of this poem.

The Way of the Land, 1967

∽

From **Parallels**

2.
Our ships on the sea,
Abraham's canopy on waves of sand—
ascents to the land.

Behind us the scrawl of colorful advertisements,
behind him an airy commandment, mighty,

loading a cloud pregnant with ghosts,
releasing particles of death.

To the rhythm of hoofbeats, Abraham plays
sounds of never.

Sand and wave, wave and sand,
the patriarch and us,
flickering and ascending.

3.

The whole land is a tree without one tree in it:
trunk of the valley, bark whitening in the wind,
boughs of the mountain riverbeds—

we grew tired as if carrying baskets,
baskets of sun.

I tell you that your beauty endures,
bending down over the thorns, looking for a well,
cracked plates in your arms—

we sang as if carrying bunches,
bunches of dew.

A boulder-choked valley rising—
we lay down, exposed in shadow the color of sky.

7.
They run carrying sand,
words heavy in my pails:

the children say hello to me.

Yossi and Eli and Tali and Tzip,
the last grain of sand on the smooth beach—
we'll bring the sea!

They run carrying water,
words flowing in my riverbeds:

the children ask me my name.

A knocking in the deep,
the last brick in the grand bridge falls—
Reuven and Robert and X.

13.
Just as Abraham assembled curtains of purple and azure,
Yossi and Tzip built in a wall's breach
where ants stumble, and I thought of long columns:

Just as a caravan of footsteps departs to be erased in sand,
Shimon and Levi climb up a trembling ladder,
picking the fruit of covenant to fill their sacks.

What can we say now? The snow melts in your eyes—
just as bees sashay about the corolla of your frost,
Sarah will recline, desired, in a tamarisk's shade.

And Abraham lifts up a handful of sand, his generations,
scattered when he leaps towards a hovering tenderness,
just as I quickly kiss the lashes of your locked eyes.

15.
The valley is quiet, narcissus erect,
a mole comes up to inhale the sun's breath,
a sun that blends variety in years.

In the wadi, the graying flotilla of summer passes,
the waterflow disappears, air waits, our eyes,
the anchor drawn up from a distant shore, set sail.

And the sun, swollen with burning hydrogen,
will redden and melt the planets as it fades away,
not you and I, not here and there — — — all one.

A dragonfly hovers over a transparent wave,
wings of silence return to a nest of dust,
the dust that will be sown with shining day.

Notes to the Poem

This sequence was completed in April 1966 and to some extent functions as a companion piece to "Ha'ir" (The City). If "Ha'ir" bade ambivalent farewell to New York City, the new sequence of fifteen poems enacted Ben-Yosef's process of setting roots in Israel, in the landscape of the northern Galilee. The title, "Haqbalot" (which I've rendered as "Parallels"), refers to parallelism, as in the poetic figure common in Psalms, but also, appropriately, contains the meaning of reception—here, Ben-Yosef's attempt to receive the landscape about him, and his hope to be received by it. In his diary, Ben-Yosef calls this "my Land of Israel poem" (1998, 78). His work here is to articulate his love of the land. Sections of the poem list types of trees and plants, anatomize sights and scents, name constellations and planets. He watches Israeli children at play, and when they ask him his name, he feels the collapse of his internal American architecture—a "knocking in the deep, / the last brick in the grand bridge falls"—and mentally reviews "Reuven and Robert and X," his Israeli name, his diaspora name, and a third cipher representing perhaps some future synthesis of the two, perhaps what can be contained in neither, perhaps even the absence of identity.

The biblical Abraham is his familiar spirit in the poem, appropriate since the patriarch was the first immigrant to the Land of Israel. Ben-Yosef revisited the trope of comparing his own migration to Israel with that of Abraham to Canaan; he also used the comparison in the first poem he wrote in Hebrew, written on Israeli Independence Day in 1960 and copied into his diary since, he wrote, "I might in some moment of emotion burn it" (1998, 8).

Ben-Yosef first took "Parallels" to the editor and critic Shlomo Grodzensky who, despite his great admiration for the young poet's ability, didn't like the poem, considering it overly difficult and obscure. Ben-Yosef explained that he purposefully did not order the poem in a clear sequence or unite its disparate elements in some explicit whole, but rather intended the experience of reading the poem to reflect the experience of "immigration to Israel, the gathering of the exiles . . . forcing the reader to engage in a similar activity of ingathering" by taking the various elements of the poem "to bring them from their dispersion and gather them in one place" (1998, 86).

Grodzensky's concerns were valid, though, since these poems, fascinating as they are, reflect the poet in transition, not yet addressing readers but instead writing to hear himself and refine what he hears. Indeed, the poem's explorations of the landscape of the northern Galilee, presented as alien and off-putting as much as beautiful and inviting, parallel the explorations of the Hebrew language itself, still a field of exploration rather than patrimony as it is for the children in the poem who "run carrying sand, / words heavy in my pails," and Ben-Yosef expressed doubt that he would repeat these efforts at modernist versions of Psalms. Another editor, Ephraim Broide of the journal *Molad*, was very enthusiastic about the poems and published them in the journal.

Incidental War: 1967

1.
One wants, as part of a war's due course,
to write singular poems, without
images like leaves and eyes and ash.

When a nation goes out in arms, to write
poems like folk songs, without similes:
No "Like autumn leaves, the bayonets . . ."

Without rhyme, such as "eyes"
And "At the machine gun / Number two will
go on, if number one dies."

A book all readers can understand,
poetic lines with no meter at all,
unlike the soldiers that fall.

2.

He didn't remember her shoulder so frail,
Nor her flowery housecoat with its bulging line
Over her growing child, nor the frail sound of her voice
As she said: only this one who isn't is all mine.

Seven months, eight? He didn't remember,
Even her delicate earlier form he forgot;
The flowers at the doorstep died, and finally
Her voice: he's all mine this one who is not.

When the burning wheel reeled on his face
Even the scent of my perfume left no sign;
There are sand dunes here, and the cry of shells:
He is mine! No, mine! No, mine!

3.

Silence in Cairo.

The residents are hiding in their homes.

Public transportation is on strike.

Even the belly dancers have stopped moving, their muslin sent to
clinics.

The Pyramids are on blackout and the Sphinx is mute.

Now the only riddles are for the officers.

This one moans, that one bangs his fist.

The people of Cairo turn to the radio that says things clearly.

A dust storm is developing in the southern desert.

In the Suez Canal a few ships were detained, but they'll soon be on
their way.

In the eastern desert the imperialists have broken through in several
places.

They'll soon be gone.

4.
And then we reached Red Sea shore.
But it wasn't red at all, not even a flower:

only sand, white in the night,
stars that had fallen by its side.

Desert constellations, so many,
sparkling on the low stretches.

Then the waves revealed a new day,
we peeled off our sweaty clothes,

and then we celebrated the end of combat
in an eternity of swelling foam:

just a stream of white all the morning,
bodies afloat upon the Red Sea.

5.

Your eyes have yet to see, yet they contain
the form of him unseen;
Your lips yet to be free, will yet explain
the tale of him untold;
Flesh of his flesh, bone of his bone,
now you are mine alone.

Your tiny body, intertwined with mine,
Will draw strength from his that is not;
And one small moment of peace will shine
Like everlasting rest;
Flesh of his flesh, bone of his bone,
now you are mine alone.

Notes to the Poem

Translated by Yehudit Ben-Yosef and Michael Weingrad.

From **In Memory of Barry Fogelson**

4.
In copper leaves I forged your voice's cell,
a vessel to bear you: a bronze root to keep
the shadows of your face, and so I quell
your death, for me at least, that dogs my sleep;
the dawn alone will rust in rising trees
that rot with green, the root withers and dries,
the stench of fallen fruit evokes unease
at my own growth: the wood revivifies.
The bark that used to be so smooth will be coarse;
hand will rock in hand; no friend is here;
and so my body, stooped and bent, will I force
to stand: spine, sinew, heart, eye, ear,
and bear this vessel that crumbles before our eyes:
so from oblivion once more a man will rise.

Notes to the Poem

This poem is one of several Ben-Yosef wrote about his friend Barry
Fogelson, who first inspired his decision to move to Israel.

From **A Night and Day of Love**

Night

3.
If only this page were like you as you sleep,
starless, without a mark: dawn's light
over a field still dark, the territory of your innocence,
the leaves reemerging from careening night,
a slow blooming into color, smell, sound,
you appear to me, a word is your appearance,
the dizziness of constellations passes, it is all
in this pulsing: your chest, my pen, a new start.
And I go up to where you lay, draw apart
the curtains over dreams that withdraw,
in the silent forests of your brow the staging ground
where my metaphors are gathered, and I shut my eyes,
born a second time in this year of destruction.

4.

A train whistles in the distance, but you will not leave
with me this time: the tracks above the waves,
bridges of smoke to there, where my desire
and laughter gather on ashen flags;
and the rustle of white dresses behind the ruined
wall, and rats squeaking in the rosebushes
testify to a familiar frost, reminding one
of dusty lamps and ancient tomes.
And the rows of headstones: a tin can, splinters
from the missing doors, nothing more, for there
is nothing but our room: dew upon the clods
in the mirror of your dreaming face, gleam
of a star upon my verses here, from where they return.

As You Get Dressed, 1969

༈

My Father Said

When I dream of a bridge, it has always been destroyed,
its columns shattered, its span of road smashed
the ends of its cables fixed only in the air,
connecting nothing between here and there.

And so I distrust poems whose themes are dreams.
A dreamer is not a thinker, and in night's ooze
what's it to him if he flies to the clouds or dives
to palaces in the sea—either way they are lies.

As a boy I lived near a mighty bridge,
and I remember flags upon it, for the age
of wars has ended, my mother said to me.
My father said: and now the world is free.

Notes to the Poem

This poem expresses Ben-Yosef's skepticism about poetry and his
parents both. The bridge, a common trope in his poems, signifies
poetry's deceptively easy ability to connect unlike things. Neither is
his parents' naïve faith in liberal internationalism to be trusted.

Moonless

By day you are land, at night
you appear without a landmark,
the waiting sea, moonless.

Haven't we said farewell? We parted
and the station lights went out,
my locomotive chuffed and left.

But here, only water, swelling
and receding in tortured throbbing,
the ancient mother breathing in the sea.

I dive down to myself,
to the seed we were
in caverns deep and sweet.

Notes to the Poem

There is a touch of Hart Crane's mystical, sexual, oceanic ambience from "Voyages" here, and in the poem "What Was Longed For" as well.

What Was Longed For

I remember depths
in the ocean that caresses longed-for shores,
sponge and coral clasping the continent's slope—

what the moon can discover
at the nape of the neck!

Also a pressure upward:
I remember sudden surges
at a new island's birth, and a silvered horizon—

you breathe and in my eyes
rise two volcanic peaks.

In the beginning, silent cells,
then worms crawl from the sea
to warm themselves, and after a billion years: birds—

singing and hovering, the moon and me,
shining and yearning.

Songs for Yehudit

Lion Sighs

I, who know your hair in sunlight,
why am I now surprised?
Does not night make of each color a symbol
and your hair, which is light,
in the dark becomes sorrow.

I knew your waist more slender than a rose—
here rests the weight of your thighs
like the warmth of roots in a wild land,
and with the full light
in his eyes, a lion sighs.

Thirsty, he gazes at the clear stream
like your braid upon the pillow,
gazes and moans, for a night without prey
is too bright, like daylight
in which he gnaws at his usual obsessions.

Lion Roars

I suffer in this span between
your fingertips and toes, a space
full of the blowing of the moon
and the call of silenced birds.

The undergrowth falls silent now,
the empty landscape tense before
the leap of a rightful, primal conqueror
chasing his fulfillment in a dreamed jungle.

And you, so fearless? This signal of
your closing eyes, as if the blessing
of your desire is spread upon the sheet, its grasses
sparkling with sweat, watered with blood.

A lion roars! Yet such thunder
echoes like a bird in a still night,
and as he falls silent, the moon will return
to reveal the marrow of the world.

Lion Sings

Rolling over on my back I see: more stars to count,
And what's this tickling in my hide?
Perhaps I've swallowed birds? But I'm a good, bird-loving soul—
So why this chirruping inside?

Birds on the wing, twittering, my battles took off flying
while you stay by my side in the night;
we fall asleep together, and in a dream we wave away
memories of a final flight.

Thus satisfied and dignified, without any movement at all,
a lion sings of the coming of rest:
from his hairy mouth, from between his jaws, there escapes the note
of a bird returning to its nest.

And now he only wants to sleep, his slackened muscles
twining in the grass and sun;
so too our bodies entangled on this sheet
in the whiteness of their strength become one.

Notes to the Poem

Ben-Yosef wrote these poems in May 1968 for Yehudit's birthday.
They constitute some of the many poems in which Ben-Yosef medi-
tates on his sexual-emotional relationship with his wife. On the one
hand, these poems express a guilty sense that a man does violence to a
woman in his sexual relationship with her. On the other, they express
an insecurity that a woman remains in some sense elusive and uncer-
tainly possessed by him.

It is difficult to do justice to the often intricate musical elegance
of Ben-Yosef's poetry at this stage in his work. For instance, the lines
I have rendered as "and as he falls silent the moon will return / to
reveal the marrow of the world" are, in Hebrew: "veyare'ah yashuv
la'asher nashav / legalot atzmot atzmut olam."

In Memory of My Living Parents

Elegies are only for the dead. And yet
a bloom may come from hollow eyes, its scent
so different, shall we say it's just the human
spirit? It's possible to sing to you
so far away without a farewell hug,
caress of graying hair, a photograph
in the mail every now and then, but only
to you as spirits, for then one can mourn
your deaths, can grieve the truth. Yet such is the world
with neither truth nor death here, just the law
of thermodynamics, even in the grave,
and to mourn you with flowers isn't what I want.

Everything is late, even the sunset—
so you told me, Mother, your hair then sun
and earth, a woman in her bloom—its light
still travels to us, eight minutes late,
years we haven't seen each other, thirty-
one years as son and parents, and never once
was I a minute early, until today,
imagining your late memory before my eyes
that yearn for a landscape of dreams and constellations,
for I was sure, that even if you cease,
you'll be remembered to the fetus in me,
and though you die my poems will be its joy.

We all remember, yet it isn't really memory
one has when anxiously attempting to seize
a living hour of life, like you, Father,
who put your heart upon the page, yearning
in secret to be another, to dwell in story,
preserved beyond the instant: you wrote about
a bird in a gilded cage, it seemed to me,
its wish for freedom, something age-old,

inscribed on ruled sheets whose lines your scrawl
escaped, your freedom never came, and now,
though you both live forever in my poem,
forever disappointed, your son is here.

You put aside your pages, Father, while I,
no longer a boy, still write, a weighty calling,
you say, yet even heavier are your image
and the lists of memory: man was created
like a star, his strength was wrenched from cosmic fire
to freeze as formless rock until the coming
of water, life, coral cells, seaweed
climbing toward the air, the mighty lizard
that chews the trees like cud, the apes too tired
to jump, the rocks in the hands of men that swarm,
multiplying in my memory, in your sighs,
Father, and, Mother, in your endless tears.

Until the year three thousand six hundred,
the weight of man in the world will be like the weight
of the world, the weight of memory will be
like the weight of precious metals, gold and silver,
like the weight of heavy elements, uranium, plutonium,
exploding, wiping out at a single blow
the past, and every living thing will rise
free, like your bird, Father, but without
the golden cage, or light, as Mother's hair
turns ever grayer in the empty room,
free on the wind, as if it really died,
open to the ultimate joy of nothingness.

Thus will you live forever, and I with you,
all of us united, as the whole earth
turns into heaven, and my poems and what's left
turn imaginary as the voices of stars,
and a waving handkerchief will not intrude

like a blindfold on our eyes, and no echo
of lines from a letter bearing greetings from
an absence, a separate existence, your hand,
Father, making for the pen, your lips,
Mother, murmuring—"ask again how
he's doing, missing him always"—
Elegies are only for the living.

From **At Twilight**

3.
Blindness, scorch of the nettle in the gulch, the undergrowth swept
by the slaughtering dryness of twilight, of all that wasn't done and
    the sun
again behind me as I return from the day's ground to this summit:
your raised thigh beneath the sheet, the fertile, intimate hilltop
and the descent to the hips without fear of the rounded slide
to the softest soil, in which a wanderer at rest can dream
to the rhyming tune of bees—you are sleeping, I won't wake you
even though my head bends thirsty to you, I won't muddy with my
    kiss
the clarity of your cheek or ripple of your lips as they breathe,
won't rouse you from your perfection lest the arid cracks
of hope pass from my brow to mar the crown in you,
known only in the taste of your forgotten dream—
though I've forgotten the taste of your shoulders and the small
    hollow
where they join the rise of your neck, the joined glow of twin
planets before the age of the flood, when it's possible
to lie down in equality of desire, waking joyfully together,
not you solitary in your slumber and me by your side like a sad
    voyeur,
my yearning cheered at the opening of your eyes, your look of fear
and failure at the ending of your dream, waking to the presence
of your lover, of the world at twilight, of the demand for mercy.

The Dead and the Loving, 1974

⤐

His Memory for a Blessing

for Barry Fogelson

May his memory be a blessing, though when
was there ever a blessing in memory? I remember
you and am reminded of your death, in a distant room
in a hospital I never saw, trapped
in tubes and valves to slow the race
of your time whose gallop
I loved. I remember myself
and am reminded of a foreign tongue, a desk
crowded with regrets, how to write in the spirit
of the paintings you never got to paint.
You made a sculpture of a branch, and I call it
a branch, for it is a sculpture of a branch.
I remember your life, and I pass through
the hardness of summer in the land you wanted
so much to come to, and through winter days
that waver in mist and pass away
like winter days. And I am reminded of nothing
but next year's narcissus,
and cyclamen, and on to the globe thistle,
to the blue thorn of the beginning of memory.

Notes to the Poem

Translated by Esther Cameron and Michael Weingrad. The phrase "his memory for a blessing" is the literal translation of "zichrono livra-khah," which follows the name of one deceased. The poem treats the final collapse of distance, imagination, and metaphor into the reality of things as they are, the identity of each thing only with itself. See the introduction for further discussion.

On a Birthday

On a birthday unlike the normal run of days
I lower the shutters, and only the book
shines, the empty page of days that come
and go, my mother who bore me and raised me
to the sky has left and won't come back, and my father
who bore my seed in joy will come to a sea
fused solid as a tombstone, and my forbearing wife
is raised in beauty's orphanhood with my soul
above the writing, through the space of life, across
the day that shines like the act of birth.

Got a pen? I hardly have time
but I'll try: name, no problem, situation
n plus 2, address, we're about to move,
and for profession I'll put a book
that will change the face of the earth,
and the salary, let it be a hundred, a thousand,
zero plus 2, my son's body like a spring
as he catches a ball, and when my daughter
spins in a dance the whole land twirls.

Throughout the days of his life, the body
is poured and cast by the soul, the hand slaps
the hard little buttock till the baby cries in pain,
so that tomorrow he glowers in battle, and his hand,
no longer soft, caresses the girl's softness,
and when the body hardens from love, he invades
a young woman who surrenders with a power
called source of all life, yet life weakens
the hand of the old man conversing with his wife
like souls on the darkening balcony, and they want to burst
from the softness of the body heavy with desire, until
he kisses her good night on her wrinkled forehead,
and the soul blooms from the cracks in the tottering body.

Notes to the Poem

The first stanza repeats versions of the Hebrew root that can mean "to bear/carry," "to raise," and "to marry": thus what I have translated as the "mother who bore me and raised me," the "father who bore my seed in joy" (itself echoing Psalm 126), and the "forbearing wife."

Anemones

Soon we shall go out once more to the anemones
pulsating in blue, in purple, and especially
in red, which to the Greeks was
the blood of one Adonis, a handsome lad, a little like
David our shepherd. But on Adonis
never fell the ire of an old and jealous king,
but rather an efficient wild boar. Others call it
the blood of flighty Aphrodite,
whose pearly foot was scratched in the wild
scramble for her gored young man.
Thus or otherwise, they speared and stabbed the youth
and turned his spilt blood into the flower I love.
When first I saw a carpet of anemones
it was upon the hills above the Sea of Galilee, at evening,
during what is called an exercise in laying mines,
but really was a bitter battle with the rocks,
using antiquated weapons known as shovels. The sun
had gone by then, and, like a full moon,
the lake was filled with an exquisite brightness,
and also from above it was a thrill to gaze upon
the blue, the purple, and especially the red
of the anemones within the practice area.
While digging, we were careful not to hurt
a single miracle, and we laid training mines
and hung the warning signs on the barbed wire,
and then stood back, the lake below us,
like the beloved's navel, from which we drink
to life, whenever not at war.

Notes to the Poem

The translation is by Curt Arnson.

The Bitter End

A man grows bitter at the end of things,
for instance: the Mediterranean Sea.
Fifteen nations line its waves
Yet somehow it all ends with me.

In three millennia, they haven't found
a coastline better made for war,
so here at the end the potsherd-lovers
can cheerfully increase their store.

If I were a laughing child, I'd dive
into a sea that was mine alone,
but at the end of Israel's twenty-third year
I defend children of my own.

Late Visit to Rosh Hanikra

From here the sea is like a map of the sea,
the sun turns iridescent in the evening, like a rainbow
or a gate. Yet the cliff is as white as ever,
its rock the color of death. Alone,
I'm even more alive returning to climb
above the rusting iron bars, above
the corridors of sea-foam, to leap to the summit,
a border of rusted wire, I alone
live. Yet from here one sees a map
not life itself, pathways leading back
to the locked gates of color, bubbles
of seventy hues that have survived dizzily
in the dance of white, while life itself is mighty,
and its meaning is to jump and dive into
the dark abyss around the island's white,
for the dead may not dive there, only I.

Notes to the Poem

Rosh Hanikra is a site on the Mediterranean coast near the town of Nahariya. It is famed for its white seaside cliff and natural grottoes. The poem captures Ben-Yosef's passion and force, love for life intertwined with consciousness of death, solitude intertwined with love. The summit he climbs to is "not life itself." Life itself is the jump into the dark abyss below.

Watchman, What of the Night

Watchman, what of the night?
Watchman, what of the day?
Watchman, what is to come?
Watchman, what can I say?
Watchman, what have I done?
Watchman, what will I be
but a watchman on guard alone
while others watch me?

Notes to the Poem

The phrase, of course, is from Isaiah 21.

The Veteran Writer Returns to His Exile

for Haim Leaf

The veteran writer returns to his exile.
Halfway up the ramp he turns to look
once more at his country, but his friends
are invisible behind the tinted glass,
and he enters the plane, satchel in hand,
his face like a manuscript erased.
He wears a coat, for it's snowing there
while crocus and narcissus bloom
in the Judean hills, and he has a hat on
for God freezes the exposed heads of Jews
in exile; he mutters to himself in Hebrew
not to forget his prayers, e.g., *shalom,*
ma nishma, todah rabah, lehitra'ot,
in the morning papers, in the TV guide,
in the donors' speeches, in trust beyond telling.

Notes to the Poem

The translation is by Esther Cameron and Michael Weingrad. Haim Leaf was a Hebrew activist, scholar, and writer who lived in the United States, where he edited the Hebrew journal *Bitsaron* and was a longtime faculty member of Yeshiva University.

Gaza Like Death

Set me as a seal upon thy heart, as a seal upon thy arm: for love is
strong as death; jealousy as cruel as She'ol: the coals thereof are
coals of fire, which have a most vehement flame. Many waters cannot
quench love, nor can the floods drown it: if a man would give all the
substance of his house for love, it would be utterly scorned.
—Song of Songs

A few hundred meters from the roadblock, it all
changes. The broad fields that bored you
with unending crops come to an end at the border
of a land of sectors. Garden patch-scratch
jackass-no-grass, camel-damn-all, this is
that booth in the wilderness, that lodge
in a garden of cucumbers, that you read
about, and about the besieged city
you hear from the soldier sitting opposite
that ten thousand were killed
in the siege of Gaza in the first world war,
the first woman you've seen since the border,
tall, straight-backed, neck like a tower
to carry the devil knows what in a basket, perhaps
you know where the temple of Dagon is,
that Samson the hero pulled down? Sectored plots,
crowded palms, sorghum, citrus, where
do they have room, when I fired in the plaza
I hit him from four meters, a volley straight
into the face, and you turn to see the same
group of soldiers gazing out the windows
at the city materializing in filth, gray and sad
she was when we parted, but I said just forty days.

The street is long when you have to guard it.
In the plaza you recognize a pine tree and a cypress.
The air is oppressive because of the flooding

of the Nile. Beside the mosque
you recognize an acacia and a willow. The storekeeper
sits in a shabby suit like before
at his desk; under the glass plate
you recognize some kind of house, also faces,
maybe family photos; the air is oppressive
because there is nothing but air in the store.
The street is long; in the long store they still keep
emptied sacks, the account books
arranged in order on the table.
In the second store they have put in new shelves
to hold a screw or two, a wrench, a hammer.
Beside the market you recognize a date palm,
and in the store across from it the air
is oppressive because of yesterday's
grenade, splinters of glass opaque with
blood. On the long street you recognize one
man, the next guard. Let him hurry up and come.

Towards evening the children play soccer
in the empty lot next to the market, where yesterday
a grenade killed a man. The children aren't men
that disappear in the crowded street. You see them
in the morning, flying kites in the wind from
the sea where you're not allowed to swim. Others bend
under baskets of melons, for it's melon season.
Others supervise, youth watches child, child
watches tot, and when you pass they shout "Yahud!"
and the tot is terrified, "Yahud!" and runs for his life
while his watchers roar with laughter. The children
are not men and you see a young girl,
yellowish in a flowered dress. A sack of sawdust
on her shoulder. Beside the candy stall she peeps
at you for a minute, her face grimy and pretty,
and puts down the sack. In her unknown tongue she pleads

and the seller refuses, the people
are not children, and you want to say
but you're not allowed to say. Anyway she has already picked up
her sack; her steps take her back to the crowded street.

You can't complain that the storekeepers are resting.
You walk and time moves forward with you, as if
the city is already familiar and its inhabitants
friends. Look, they're smiling at you
from the workshop in which with Oriental suppleness
they work wonders weaving wicker chairs.
If not for the Uzi you'd be a tourist; you sip
coffee in the alley next to the plaza, linger
before the mosque, admire the breadth of the carpets
inside the sanctuary. Here in Samson's day
stood a statue of a fish, and in the market you saw a shark
they caught in the waters near here. If only
you could say to all these nice people,
come, let's go for a swim. All of us naked and
something falls on the street and they quickly scatter
and you see the car passing in slow motion
and you're behind a column in that prolonged
fraction of a second before the explosion and you run
with other soldiers running and shooting down the
long empty street where we suffered no casualties.

A night of curfew and peepholes. You might say
eyeless except that you see in your nightmare
the crouching beggar rise and pull out a dagger.
Shut houses, unknown alleys, peepholes.
On the base it's hard to sleep during the day because
of the flies. And at night those not on guard see
a movie, the kind with girls lying
legs apart and men playing marbles.
They peer from every peephole, you can feel it.

The horse-faced company commander brings
flies in after him and it's hard to sleep, but at night
legs open slowly, not like peepholes
that suddenly open fire. Every house is a wall
and overhead, behind a red curtain
the last light of the curfew goes out. Anyone not awake
at night opens his eyes on girls
spreading their legs and waiting for the slow rolling
marble to bull's-eye inside them.
You say don't check the peepholes
and put on a beggar's blind face. For the company commander
chewed out the diligent platoon commander
who shot and wounded a woman last night.
Though he didn't reprimand him officially.

Only at night, sitting on the roof, facing the sea,
you remembered a woman in a free land, devoted,
slender as a stalk in the wide fields of grain; here
on this street it's hard to imagine. The air is scorched today.
Heat waves in the shape of girls in black passing by,
baskets on heads; beneath their garments of mystery
flash plastic sandals. What are they
afraid of? There are no men to look at them.
There are no men in Gaza, only sudden explosions
as though with women they know no repose.
At night, above the villas along the coast
you remembered that you have a woman whose thighs
lift to you like those dark waves
uncovered and smooth. The men in Gaza are sullen,
and the villas of the elite along the coast
decorated in soft pastel hues. Don't look at women.
All the same, one comes by as if she just
came up from the desert, a face of sweet dates,
body hinted in the wind. But you have a wife,
and in the villas along the coast there's no lack of money.

On the last day, because of a bullet that blazed
among the gravestones, you're forced to learn
one more history lesson: three hundred
suspects in the schoolyard, a suitable place
for a prison. The lucky ones picked up first
sit in the shadow of the wall, the rest cover
their heads with handkerchiefs. The sun is still hot
even though Bedouin tents were unloaded. You allow
the boys of army age to go to the faucet.
Were they the ones who rebelled with a solitary shot
at the half-track going through the darkened graveyard?
The security personnel check their documents, looks as though
no shot was fired, the half-track didn't go down
to search between the gravestones for nothing, and the joke
was not so funny: Hey!
What's all the noise up there? You allow
a young man, who is certainly
the father of a family, to approach and drink.
The sun is still burning, but the heat has escaped
from these stony faces to the graveyard
where a half-track full of laughing soldiers is racing along.
What's all that noise up there? Shut up! For God's sake!

The statue-faced company commander congratulates you
on the capture of the terrorists and that's that, forty days,
the troop carrier turns north, you have escaped death
where a blind man was buried under rubble of idols.
Idolatrous love is beautiful as the sand, comely
as the summer sky, terrible as a wall with peepholes.
But the company commander is satisfied and that's that,
you weren't killed and didn't do much killing. The troop carrier
speeds through palm trees, sorghum, citrus where
there's room for ten cows and a chicken coop, last year
I planted flowers. Nearing the roadblock
you suddenly long for open fields, like

I told you, it passes quickly, wide spaces that
continue till Rehovot, I'll get off and go on foot.
A few hundred meters from the roadblock it all
comes back and you want to say of the army
it taught me one thing: a man's way of life is like his land.
And the stall at Yad Mordechai is still selling honey.

Notes to the Poem

Translated by Yehudit Ben-Yosef and Esther Cameron. The title plays on the word *azah*, which can mean both "Gaza" and "strong." This poem deals with Ben-Yosef's experiences during reserve duty in the Gaza Strip, which he also treated in prose fiction in the novel *Mirmah*. When Ben-Yosef participated in a 1977 conference of Jewish and Arab writers, he read this poem to the assembly and found that there was interest in translating the poem into Arabic.

Voices in Ramah, 1976

❧

Soldier's Prayer

my god may it be your will that i return
to my home in peace with peace for all israel
my god may it be your will that i return
to my home in peace with peace for my god
may it be your will that i return to my home
in peace with peace my god may it be your will
that i return to my home in peace with my god
may it be your will that i return to my home
in peace my god may it be your will that i return
to my home my god may it be your will that i
return to my god may it be your will that
i return my god may it be your will
my god may it be my god
my god

Notes to the Poem

The poem is a horrifying rush in which the repeated prayer fractures and fuses as words drop out before what may be the death of the supplicant. Israeli novelist Aharon Meged told Ben-Yosef that the poem deserved inclusion in Israel's secular liturgical canon.

On the Basalt of the Golan Heights

for Anadad Eldan

From within your lake of night, its waves turning blue,
you asked if I would write of the basalt
of the heights, you who sought to wander to Dan,
that I who return from Tel Hara through Nahal
Haki, the village of Jiora, and ruined Quneitra
should write about basalt, igneous poems
the sound of which you never saw at Sinai—
what can I say, my friend, all places have their poems,
all hearts, erupting then cool, are equal
on the Great Kibbutz, and in the meantime we left
the wreckage beneath extinct volcanic peaks, skeletons
of fighter jets planted on the plain, snows of hope
covering each form, erupting then cool, as if
nothing grey existed any more, not basalt
and not the fragments like it,
resembling stones for God's slingshot
only smaller and sharper,
like the image of man.

Notes to the Poem

The poem is dedicated to the poet Anadad Eldan, a poet of the Palmach generation (born in Poland in 1926) whose latest collection of poems appeared in 2014.

On the Eternal Mission

"A nation with an eternal mission" was
written in Arabic on what had been the gate
of what had been the Syrian camp in El Al,
and from there we continued under bombardment
to Ramat Magshimim, a Jewish town overlooking
ancient ruins, crosses etched in the basalt,
and at the bend in the road we saw another Syrian tank
abandoned, very modern, disguised in reeds
as if it were embarrassed by its mission,
and from there we continued under bombardment
to the hill we received as an inheritance
in the days of Og, King of Bashan—on the very same day,
as I learned later from a news broadcast after the battle,
that the Syrians invaded Ramat Magshimim
and desecrated the Torah scroll in the synagogue there—
we continued under bombardment to the hill
on which Jews were killed, Jews whom the Syrians call
Crusaders, and the Crusaders called Christ-killers,
and Christ doesn't call anything,
for he still hasn't begun his eternal mission.

Notes to the Poem

The Arabic slogan seen on the gate of the military camp was common in Syrian state propaganda.

On the Readiness for Sacrifice

Greater than the readiness for sacrifice
is the compulsion to cry, for thou shalt not cry
when the field of thorns along the road
ignites and burns with hisses and bursts,
spraying shrapnel because of the munitions there,
until a young soldier runs from his position
to the reservist's half-track and grabs an extinguisher
to shoot foam on the field that burns anyway,
and across the road lie the dead. Greater than
the readiness for sacrifice is the urgency
of rage, for thou shalt not scream when a kid
sobs over his dead friend, hugging
his weapon and gazing heavenward
as if he knows that the chopper will come
rising from the Galilee, and from the hilltop
they alert your vehicle that the enemy is back,
two tanks in front of your slender cannon.
And greater than the readiness for sacrifice
is the eagerness for slaughter, for thou shalt not
have mercy when your gunsights close in
and your finger launches small shells to drive
the enemy from the land, yet you have to stop
when the tanks flee and your track is quiet and you
gaze heavenward and know that there is nothing
greater than the readiness for sacrifice.

Notes to the Poem

Like the preceding two poems, this comes from Ben-Yosef's experiences in the Yom Kippur War.

Noon in Jerusalem, 1978

&

The Deeds of the Fathers

The deeds of the fathers are a sign for the sons,
yet a son is permitted to ask the nature of the deed
and the father is obligated to say, it is because of this
that the world did for me when I went out of the world
to go forth to a mountain and another mountain and another
in the wilderness of freedom, to improve our standing as we go
with fire before me as it was in all the dwellings
of our generations, desiring my allegiance
to the future, sons moving under cover
on a mountain and another and another in a wilderness glad
with acacia and myrtle, criss-crossing roads, houses—
I've grown tall, says the father on the balcony, yet my son
will grow taller than me. And the only sad thing is this,
that the one who cries "follow me" doesn't make it any easier
for the one who comes after, he only calls behind him
be strong, as I do every morning to my son:
be strong in your studies, in your games,
be brave enough to breathe the living air.

Notes to the Poems

This poem plays on several texts, including the Exodus story as
narrated in the Passover seder. The poem alters the traditional expla-
nation to the children during the seder (Exodus 13:8): "It is because
of this that the Lord did for me when I went out of Egypt." Another

phrase, "follow me," is from Israeli military culture in which the offi-cers traditionally lead their men into battle.

Letters to America

1. Letter to My Brother

I write to you with simple words,
because you do not understand Hebrew.
We share no language, and yet perhaps
some brotherly bond exists that strives, across
the mighty waters, to touch, so that
one of these days, in one of these lands,
you'll see that you have not yet reached your self.

I write to you because you do not understand,
and yet you want to be my brother,
not like those wandering relatives that every Jew
has somewhere else in the world, but my own flesh
and blood, your lack of self resounding
in my very bones, and didn't you once say,
"From this sad distance I'm proud of you."

I write to you because you do not want to be,
my brother. The king's image has left you, and nothing
remains but a clean hand on a glass stem,
wine by the sea, a holiday, your eyes gazing east
with longing, your mouth swallowing, your heart
aching, softly beating, how pleasant it is
to think of one's blessings, to relax in reverie.

How good it is—*hinei mah tov*—to bear your pain
inside you, dry all the while, with salt and wine
in your eyes, and the horizon revolving like a gear
from evening to morning and back again. Come back again,
my brother, stop yearning and read what is written.
These simple words I write to you, your brother
who lives on the Street of the Watchman, in Israel.

2. Letter to My Sister

To my sister, captive among the gentiles,
to my sister, snatched from us, no one the wiser,
I write on a slate as smooth as the skies,
a reflection of cloud and the burning sun,
a banished brother's message, because your many addresses
have been lost to me since you turned to gentile ways.

To my sister, younger than me by ten years,
to the baby whom I never knew, to the schoolgirl
who wrote to me from over the sea, "I fear
that I will not be what I want to be."
I am the sole witness of your captivity,
for our parents permitted you all, all those years.

To my sister who, when pure, was permitted to all,
to my sister whose purity can never again be believed,
who wrote to me, "I hope that you are well
but not wealthy," only I can weigh your worth,
diamond and pearl, witness of your soul within,
because no one can have faith that your faith can be pure.

To my sister who wrote, "I can no longer trust
my parents, I fear I will not be fulfilled
in my life, I hope that you are well
but not wealthy," I want to write a poem
but you have been captive, your addresses lost
for so long, and I am the witness that they are gone.

3. Letter to My Mother

Length of days: Mother, can you give me this?
Because I would write you all the honor—*kol hakavod*—
that we harvest here, as distant from you
as a vineyard from wine, as the gleaming grape on the vine
from the dull glass in your hand, as you stand alone in the night.

Where are you now, Mother, alone in the night?
Because I would speed to you all of the trembling
that shook me in the bombardments on the Golan, a new revelation
at a smoking mountain for your son who played with toys in time
of crematoriums, a child of war who never cried for his mother.

Only now, only here in this land, did I ever cry
for my mother. So can you give me length of days? A blessing
in exchange for glory? For the earth here is quite full of our glory,
our watchmen-sons, and as a brave son I too would embrace
my mother with me with my people until the length of days.

But you have set sail to the end of the sea and the length of days,
yet you do not arrive at the dead or the living, not husband
or home, your grandchildren playing here in the sun.
Where are you now, Mother, alone in the light?
What is the color of your hair, above the salt waves?

4. Letters to America

My father is not here. He is in the Diaspora,
dispersed in every river and ocean.
In the seas and the lakes. In wood. In stone.
My father who yearned to sail the waves,
and finally did. We never managed to be close,
and now as I scan his letters I find the sentence,
"Letters cannot really express the deepest things."

And so I must write letters to America.
For my father was born there, and bore me there too,
And if I with my name, the gift of my father, am no more,
and my father is perished, then I must truly go down
to the depths, and try to draw up seeds
of wisdom, such as the following: "I want to encourage
my son in his quests, so he does not forget
repressed emotions and ideas, memories and fear."

And it is important to write letters to America.
Because 6 million Jews are there, less one,
6 million alive, more or less like the number
consigned to the flames in my childhood
far from the old, forgotten world, led to their deaths
in railway cars while I as a boy played on the wall-
to-wall carpet with electric trains, the gift of my father.

My father is not there. He is in the Diaspora,
all of it, all of him, and I cannot gather
the seeds of wisdom that have truly dissolved.
I can only remember and fear: a dream of my father
as Joseph, who solved the symbols of kine and corn,
and when I awoke he was dead, dispersed
in mighty waters, carried away from the place
of his own solution, the hard kernel of America.

5. A Memory of Towers

In New York City, towers soar through the air.
When I was eight, towards the end of the war,
one of our own bombers flew into a tower
by accident, destroying some of the higher floors.
And from where I was I could hear the blast,
the only one I remember from the war,
and fourteen lives were lost in that office in the sky.

At that very moment, I was in a different office,
a psychiatrist's, for my mother sought an explanation
for some matter unclear to me, some aberration
like a cough—I remember that I would cough
when I read about tubercular composers
and I loved to play music, to draw out a melody
that would rise in the bright air between towers.

For the air was still clear in those days.
Yet a plane crashed into a tower
from whose summit you could see fifty miles
and the doctor gave me a couple of games
and asked me what I liked to do,
and Mother jumped up and asked what was that noise,
until the radio reported the disaster and the end of the war.

Yet later on when I said I'm no longer a child
who would immigrate to lullaby land, but rather
am ready for Jerusalem, my mother rang up
that same psychiatrist and he asked her again
what I liked to do, for no other mother in NYC
had a son whose soul soared so through the air
and her voice rose up and crashed into the towers.

6. Letter to a Father

Like father, like son, but what is the fate of a son
with no name, with no father to whom he can write a letter?
So I write my art to a father who art in heaven,
in sky, in clouds that reap water from the sea
to sweeten the glass of ripened wine from sun-kissed vine
to my lips, like a son who secretly kissed his father.

Like wisdom, like will. But what is the fate of wisdom
when there is no longer a father to will the reply
to a letter? I study the silence of stone, the mother
of dust in which father and son embrace, and I wanted
my father's embrace, even as *av* and *ben* in Hebrew embrace
to make *even*, the stone that gives birth to them both.

Torah and a trade. Both are the birthright of a father
dearer than bread, greater than all the grains
of wisdom of a man who would dissolve into the sea.
And a son is commanded to merit what he inherits, but what
can a father bequeath that is not in the land of our fathers?
What is a father without a son, a son relieved of his command?

Like ethics, like death. But what is the ethical will
left me by my dead father, who told me, "Here
among the steel and glass buildings of New York
there are no grass and trees, no ancient rabbinic homilies,
outdated pretexts from the past. Here every man
is commanded to take sole responsibility for himself."

7. A Book for My Brother's Daughters

On the mountains of Bether, so it is written,
on mountains of spices, from the cleft in the rock
to the hills of myrrh, the beloved skipped in Solomon's song.
And songs that are skipped by rich American uncles
I'll sing to you, your uncle who lives in the land of the hart
that broke forth in the song, your father's brother with his heart
in the air, to you the heirs of that other Jerusalem
over the sea, the Zion of smoke, New York on the map,
a street with no name, only a number on a snow-covered sign.

I never played there as a child, for the neighborhood
was plied by Germans; there was even a book
with the name of your numbered street, about a spy,
an agent of the mass murderer whom you learned of,
as you learned of Babylon, Rome, and Jerusalem,
from books. It's hard to hate what we haven't seen.
The hart on the altar profaned, the sword, asphyxiation
and anguish, they fade beneath the Christmas tree; no doubt
the neighborhood improves as the Jews are taken away.

I am trying to write a new Song of Songs for you.
But where have you gone, O daughters, the uncle asks,
where have you turned on winter streets, and I try
to hide the holiday joy that breaks from the night,
coercive baubles hanging on a lit-up evergreen.
We will lie down in frost, it is written, and rise in vineyards
to drink our cup directly from the vine of earth,
with heaven's blessing and all the seas become one.
The uncle is trying to love across mighty waters.

In spring, you go out in ease to the continent's edge.
Not in fearful flight you go to welcome the sea.
And your father will buy you a present, yet for nothing
you're sold to the season, the resurrection at the shore,
the horizon empty, clean of all ships. Where have you turned,

116

O builders of Jerusalem, the uncle asks, and am I
in your hearts as I dwell on my mountain in the sky?
It's hard to love what we haven't seen. Are you
beautiful, my brother's daughters, dolls in the smoke?

8. Letter to Myself

When contact is lost and relations estranged
I relate to myself, the bonds of love, you say,
of self-confidence, after all, to be loved, to delight
in caresses received from another was always your vice,
at the very first smile from your mom and your dad
in the old neighborhood, in your cradle of gold you laughed
as if floating on waves of bliss. But I'm wary
of smiles, suspicious of uncertain joy.

You didn't hide, yet you denied your yearning,
you wanted their touch, father and mother and siblings,
and you the oldest, a master of dreams on Sunday mornings,
when the family sat and talked together, I conjured a country
where dad would work less and mom would be happy.
They didn't understand yet who wouldn't prize
such a son dreaming with open eyes for a touch?
But I don't remember these childhood scenes.

You do but you'd rather forget. Their eyes hung
like lanterns in the tunnel of night, and you moving on
when I stopped suspecting, bent over to dig up
the precious subconscious clay for strangers
who went away long ago. You refuse to acknowledge
the fact that you were loved, for I want to continue
all by myself, inviolate along the walls,
drawing near to Jerusalem and everything in it.

You desire a future for the sake of separation,
for the glittering gold of your imaginary sorrow,
or else you'd be as poor as a church mouse. I detest
my poverty as much as I love to remember
my mother waving to me, so long as I don't
return to the bars of my crib in which I floated,
as you describe it to yourself, on waves of bliss,
as if bliss waved to me from America.

9. Memories of the Tropic Zone

In winter we'd migrate south like birds,
on Christmas vacation flying down the road,
the capitol a distant vision of white domes,
and on to a land of swamps and shacks
still standing after the war in the South
that liberated myriads of slaves, and on
to Florida, two weeks of sand and sun.

The birds of New York never went so far,
but we sang and we rested, not minding the waves
that rose from some point between east and west
till they conquered the shore, the stretch of sand
allowed to the Jews, who multiplied so
in America after the war so that you could hear
Yiddish spoken there in the sunshine.

And seagulls hovered, and tiny birds
ran back and forth with the tide, almost touching
the foam. I built with my pail, I fell in love
with a mighty castle, real to me, with a wall
and a gate that seemed to have closed forever,
for I never saw anyone inside, though I spent all day
at its wall of sand until it was flooded by the sea.

Only when years went by was I able to enter
a similar castle, a house my parents bought
in Florida, with a wall of white and a gate that opened,
for I was called from Israel to my father,
lying ill, to see him one last time. Yet I believe
we'll meet again in Jerusalem on a day when the sea
will resound with the joyful song of countless birds.

10. Second Letter to My Brother

If I write again perhaps you'll understand,
for now you are both brother and colleague: I received
your book and read it, but so far you only receive
my books, and on a shelf by diplomas certifying
a foreign nation's wisdom, you've laid your brother
to rest, to gather dust at the feet of idols
in your air-conditioned study, a rare artifact,
a paper mummy preferable to a rotting corpse.

It's hard to recall that as kids we shared a room,
each morning we'd talk about school, each night about trains
that went to the ends of the land, about the ocean.
You stayed in New York, while I'm on the Street of the Watchman
who stays in the land whose language doesn't speak
to you, a land the poet of America called "Syria,"
among a people into whom the poet of England
stuck a cruel and miserly heart.

I am the man whom your Waste Land poet
described as a rat beneath the piles, carrying plague
in the world, yet who knew not a thing of the world
I carry in me, and which will not speak to you
unless you listen, unless cords of sympathy still exist
despite the quarrels over various toys, for together
we grabbed the trains that sped to the ends of the land,
to the sea, the source and end that are never full.

But I can't keep obeying the law of the land when you don't
have a land, only air mail, and I won't grant your letters' petition
for distant sympathy, when I alone am asked
to listen to your childhood across that source and end.
I carry the present, beneath the piles of the piers
of New York: with a voice like the gnawing of a rat,
like the chirp of a desert bird in expanses of sand,
like a prayer whispered on the mountain, far from the sea.

11. A Whisper to My Sister's Children

A good mother. A good mother immersed in the water.
A good mother immersed in the water and drowned.
A mother no more. A good mother no more.
For she drowned her children. Can you hear me,
my sister's children? She drowned the children
in her womb. A person takes pity on those
who might drown in the sea, yet her good soul sank,
and you, her children, along with her soul.
You, had you lived, would be her soul.

So now the mother has no soul. My sister's house
is cut off like a cross cut from western forests.
She has sworn to her captors to refuse her loving kin.
Her husband walks beneath wooden beams
and a dog barks outside. And under her husband's beard
the cherubs smile and an oiled wheel hums,
for the husband sees visions of destruction.
Thus is my sister sworn; she has dedicated her soul
to save the souls of children by ending her own.

Can you hear me, my sister's children? I am the watchman
who stays on guard, I have wine without blood,
and bread for you that is better than mourning,
that will bring you to life in the land if only you'd cross
over to me, and give up the mother
who was never a mother to you. But how
will you live beneath skies of mercy in an empty house
full of the barking of the dog outside, who guards
lest the uncle get in with his whispers of mercy.

For I will not take pity, says the body to the soul,
I will not sustain a soul that refuses to make life.
Everything ends, says the body, yet life continues
after the end of the soul. Did you hear me,
my sister's children? And do you hear me, sister?

I'm whispering to your children in the land of the living.
I take pity on your soul, for it was swept away
in the flood of captivity, and a good mother drowned,
who drowned her children out of compassion.

12. Letter upon the Waters

One who casts a letter upon the waters
will receive flowers and fruit, grass at the edges
of the vineyard, drunk on the sun, and all this
an answer to what was written on a night watch
on a vigil of grief, what flows on to the sea
that will not be split a second time, but carries tears
to sweeten the heavens. For what is a sea
if not water yearning for a land of joy.

And the rain is sweet. But only for one who doesn't
discard the image of the king, neither in dream
nor in the morning, among the wakeful vineyard rows,
at dawn whose hope is stronger than a dream
for the war is delayed, and life flourishes
on the secure borders of the possible,
the infant walks, the boy drives, the man
takes flight over the treetops to nourish his roots.

A place where the waters return to sweeten it all.
Where the sea, stretched out for others, is ready
to gather tears and the grains of wisdom
of a vanished man. Everything runs to the sea.
My mother too, who went out to sail on the current.
And my brother who hugs the shore but listens
to breakers, always coming close to him
till they jump back with a broken heart.

And all who return from our land by ship
reach only a heart of tears, and rain in the sea
is nothing but more sorrow, that will not be split
a second time. My sister is like the sea,
she holds out her arms for a moment then pulls them back
to the depths. And every letter upon the waters
were better to send directly to the sky.
A letter upon the waters will dissolve.

13. A Memory of My Father

When I came from Israel to my ailing father,
it was the first time in my life that I set foot
in a palace, a house my parents bought
with a wall and a gate, in the tropics of America.
And after I kissed my distraught mother
and then my father, I went off to sleep.
I was tired, and I never saw my father again.

He suffocated in his sleep that night. The air
of New York was the killer, my mother said.
Because of that they had fled to the tropic zone,
but there wasn't a cure there for lungs, only a doorway
in the white wall of a castle without prince or princess,
for my brother stayed up north, my sister went west,
and I live over the sea on a mountain in the air.

But even a palace without princes needs a will,
and my father willed himself to be distributed.
Relatives arrived, and some of my parents' acquaintances
borrowed a motorboat from the locals,
the kind of boat I wanted as a boy,
that could cut across the sea. But this time it was clear
that one can't go far with borrowed vessels.

So we didn't go far, but we each mumbled something,
and my sister sang, and I thought of the verdict
of the father of tribes about the few and evil
days of his life, and my mother howled Joseph
and scattered his remains on the waves, good-bye Joseph
and she dispersed his ashes, until we came
to the land that no longer knew his name.

Notes to the Poem

This poem is also discussed in the introduction. The poem is
written in iambic pentameter with a wealth of internal rhyme and

allusiveness. I will note here a few of the references that are most evident in the original.

Poem 1: *How good it is—hinei mah tov.* The line makes ironic reference to the verse from Psalm 133, sung in a number of popular Israeli folk-song versions: "Behold how good and pleasant it is for brothers to dwell together."

Poem 2: *captive among the gentiles.* The reference is to the halakhic concept of a person raised by non-Jews, and whose possible violations of Jewish law are therefore considered unintentional.

Poem 3: *all the honor—kol hakavod.* The phrase *kol hakavod* literally means "all the honor" or "all the glory," but is used colloquially to mean something like "well done." The phrase "the earth is quite full of our glory" plays on the traditional praise that the earth is full of God's glory, and full of buried soldiers who have fallen in battle.

Poem 4: *who solved the symbols of kine and corn.* The original Hebrew has Joseph as *ba'al hashever b'shefa*, the master of abundant provisions, but *shever* can also refer to interpretation, as of dreams.

Poem 5: *towers soar through the air.* The phrase *migdalim porhim ba'avir* is a talmudic phrase concerning the application of purity laws to an object in the air, here used to mock psychoanalysis.

Poem 6: *Like father, like son.* The original is "If there is no father, there is no son," a formulation that, with the phrase "Torah and trade," refers to Pirke Avot 3:21: "If there is no Torah, there is no worldly means; if no worldly means, no Torah." The poem further refers to the discussion in BT Kiddushin concerning the obligations of a father to his son's education and well-being.

Poem 7: *for nothing / you're sold to the season.* Cf. Isaiah 52:3: "For thus saith the Lord, Ye have sold yourselves for nought; and ye shall be redeemed without money."

Poem 8: *the bonds of love, you say, / of self-confidence.* The Hebrew lines strongly echo Hosea 11:4, "I drew them with cords of a man, with bands of love."

At the Desert's Edge, 1981

≪

At Twilight

Years ago in another place I wrote "At Twilight,"
on seeing the light descending like a flood
on a violent world, when only at twilight comfort
came to the Noah that I seemed to be, returning
to a woman whose thigh beneath the sheet was like
a fertile, intimate hill, and I sought to bring deeds,
children, father and mother, from a world erased.

And I've brought them this far in a sealed book.
Each book is a place, and moves about sealed in the land,
in the eternity of many places. Yet now I wouldn't go
inside at twilight but out to the rocks,
to the distant mountains, the many women in my wife,
the children filling the horizon, and I would sail
at twilight saying all my deeds will I lay here.

Notes to the Poem

This poem meditates upon Ben-Yosef's earlier poem of the same
name.

In the Light of Black Marble

Margarethe Herzl died, that is, fell victim,
in Theresienstadt, so I read in a foreign book
and couldn't believe it, in small print, in the footnotes
about her father, known in Hebrew
as Binyamin Ze'ev, in the year 1943 according
to the Christian calendar, in the Nazi camp, the daughter
of Theodor Herzl among the murdered, I didn't want to believe it.

And I went to Yad Vashem, on the slope of Mount Herzl
where her father is buried. It turned out nothing was recorded
about his daughter in Thereisenstadt. Only those victims
who had survivors in the land of the living
to testify, to declare the death of their relatives
were recorded. And no one had brought up
the memory of Margarethe. Of course I could
have told the clerk, but did not want to.

I turned to ascend. There, on the hilltop, what dominates
is the black marble monument garlanded with roses,
and one name engraved on it: Herzl. Margarethe
was born on the twentieth of May, according to the book,
on the foreign date of my daughter's birth, but not
on the Hebrew date, the nineteenth of Iyar, in Kiryat-Shmonah
in the state of Israel in the light of black marble.

Notes to the Poem

  The translation is by Esther Cameron.

Enemies

Our enemies are dead, and we want peace.
Our enemies live, and they conquer our home.
But there are also tourists, like the Christian
speaking German at the Jaffa Gate. When I walked by
slowly and with exceeding politeness, he cursed
and called me a damned Jew, for I tainted his path
into the Church of the Sepulchre. Dead are the enemies.
We need to call on the nation, to understand the new
beauty that blooms in our land in these golden times
like the tiara of gold that Rabbi Akiba gave to his wife
in exchange for her hair, which being poor she had sold
for his sake, long before the war and the iron comb.
Our enemies are dead, yet they conquer our home.

The Western Wall

You wouldn't be able to use the stones of this place
as a pillow for your head, for the stones are heavy
and the place is heavier still, and your head is heavy
with dreams of the sand that you crossed on the way
to the Mitla pass, the Eastern Wall they called it,
but we only found a signpost on a side road
leading to a lost valley, an artillery position perhaps,
whose memory we guarded with our tanks.

I see doves dwelling in the clefts of the wall,
reviewing the scraps of paper placed by Jews
on holy days, to fix the interpretations of dreams
that go up and down, and the doves moan: hoo-hoo,
who knows where is the Wall in the Sinai desert,
hoo-hoo, hooray the war is over, and the Wall
is only sand, and ever since then, we dream
of the stones of the place we call peace.

Notes to the Poem

Among the allusions are several to the episode of Jacob's dream
in Genesis.

The Murdered Song

> The gentiles believed, while we who were to be killed did not believe . . .
> Blessed are we because we did not believe . . . Because of the image of
> God in us we did not believe . . .
>
> —Yitzhak Katznelson

In other words, he said, I don't believe that Man
would on his own exterminate every Jew, surely
something will remain, a shadow of that image
they cultivated over thousands of years,
those faces shining with peace,
even in the streets of Jerusalem,
where once again the people will arise and triumph.

In other words, he said, I don't believe in our world
alone, a world that could go on without the Jewish race;
after all hadn't I managed to hide
the "Song of the Murdered Jewish People,"
many years ago, by a miracle, beneath a tree;
surely readers will remain in the rooms of Jerusalem,
to dig beneath roots for pure treasure.

And that same talent wrote, "Of all that is dear
only my heart in me remains," years before that too
was burnt; in other words, he said, I don't believe
in what has no body, so if the takers of bodies
take mine too, then I have created books for Jews,
and surely some will remain on the shelves of Jerusalem,
all beating like hearts: listen to the murdered song!

Notes to the Poem

Yitzhak Katznelson was a Yiddish and Hebrew poet and drama-
tist, active in literature, theater, and education even during his impris-
onment in the Warsaw ghetto, from which he eventually escaped to
France only to be later deported. His wife and two of his children

were murdered in Treblinka, and he was murdered in Auschwitz with his remaining son. He hid the manuscript for his Yiddish poem the "Song of the Murdered Jewish People" by burying it under a tree from where it was recovered after the war.

Poems in a Churning World, 1989

☙

On a Theme by Yitzhak Katznelson

On a silent night, with no worry of winds,
in Jerusalem's darkness that is kind to dreamers,
in the heart of the new housing, its walls
colored stones, and its shutters pulled down demurely, pine
and cedar its guardians, and smooth lawns, and flowers,
only he who keeps on until late, deep and hearkening,
he who remains to read or reflect, hears
the thundering voices of the tailor and his spouse,
trudging the street and shouting in their language of then,
from a place of Jews like briars and thorns, shouting
one to another as though over an abyss, but look
and you'll see them together, crowded in the middle of the street,
a couple, dwarfish and stout, and in their shouting
you won't hear any hint of a plea, perhaps it's a dispute
or perhaps just a discussion between Jews like briars and thorns
in the heart of the new housing, its walls
colored stones, in Jerusalem's darkness that does well
with dreamers on a silent night.

Notes to the Poem

 This translation is by Yehudit Ben-Yosef.

In a Dry Winter

An American tourist in Jerusalem bought a painting
from a young artist in Yemin Moshe and thinking
it would be lovely to hang on the eastern wall
of his living room at the end of the west, went back
and changed its title which he didn't understand:
Sambatiyon. Stones springing from a field of blue
and the white of arid exile around, stones soaked
with thirst against a background of celestial water
and the emptiness of creation below, stones yearning
for sabbath rest, the promise of the world's Creator
to life, to silence, to all the oppressed. But the tourist
called the painting he had purchased *Jerusalem*.

And I sit before my paintings in Jerusalem,
trying to remember only the future, this year
a year of drought, and tourists come to see
the good of the land, to breeze through the north,
cast an envious glance at still-empty spaces in the Negev,
for evil comes from on high, the leaves fold up
withered on their dry branches, too weak to fall,
and no wind blows to make them fall
but like tourists' fingers before the wall
they hang in space, only pointing.

I admit that I have tried to paint the sabbath,
the one that still hasn't come, for we were as dreamers
learning to will that it be no dream,
and the one who is whole never dreams.
I wanted to paint the holiness beyond the wall,
my face not like the wandering moon
that gropes the cracks to check if the dew is gathered
drop by drop, coalescing into rain, but like the face
of mother and father and uncle and aunt, tourists

who came back to stroll forever in the hills of Jerusalem,
and to feel with the serenity of stones the sabbath peace.

Yet little by little it really seems that it's possible
to believe that this is not a crazy dream,
that we're not just a fairytale in Jerusalem
but as we wish to be, a desire that flows to the horizon
and colors the faces of all the children of Israel
with the future, like a good wall stronger than the Sambatiyon,
and in a dry winter, resembling a deprived childhood,
I'll sit and paint the faces of the living people of the land
at the wall, to say, as my offering to the tourist: come
and see your children's children, in sabbath rest,
for then peace will come to all Israel, if you come
all the days of your life, then those days will come too.

Notes to the Poem

The Sambatiyon is a mythical river in Jewish folklore that would
throw boulders in order to prevent anyone from crossing it, and beyond
which the Ten Lost Tribes and the Messiah were said to reside. Yemin
Moshe is a neighborhood in Jerusalem.

On the Watershed

At the edge of the western reaches of Jerusalem,
on a cloudy day, not-quite-rain on the horizon,
through the pine needles of the forest, you can observe
the meeting of rivers that go down to the sea, the Refaim
approaching from the south and turning, joining
the Sorek from the north that overtakes and gathers
the Zanoah and the Kesalon and the Harel and Timnah and Ekron
and Gamaliel, all falling weakly down to Yavneh
by the sea, where an ancient harbor once existed,
now with a tar sand beach where it's forbidden to swim.
I haven't been there in years, since I moved up here
to Jerusalem, which stands on the watershed forgetting
the young woman's body stretched out so happy
when she slides a fragment of stone over her smooth thigh,
when she presses the conch to her ear, to hear the caps
of the tide whispering charms over her breasts;
for years I haven't lingered on sunny stretches
because I wanted to rest while memories are stored
in the closet, and only our eyes shine
amid the pine needles, to see and to suffer.

To suffer and to strive, hearts well-versed in yearning
how will they not quiver before a horizon of clouds
on a day that might be rainy or merely blurred,
how will they lay down the tablets of our sad yearning
in the capital over the watershed, our city whose common folk
are already like cantors and our cantors like scribes
and our scribes like wise men whose wisdom falls weakly
for it doesn't seek or beseech the heavens,
and suddenly you observe the rivers meeting below,
by a ruined harbor where a young woman stretches out
and slides a stone over her body's charms and sighs,

and over her breasts the sea foam whispers, in a memory
of the joy of her body's curves, the caress of her sigh.

But there is no rest even for the tablets in the ark,
for suddenly the rain returns, a cloud comes
to shroud the remains of the pier, the sea foam receding
from the silence of the failing rivers, and fragments shine
on the tip of every needle, like the diadem of a groom,
or on the late spring flowers, like the crown of a bride,
living water that will flow to Jerusalem,
and from the ark hearts will rise and look to the east,
to Kidron Vale, to the flame that rises from the depths
of the eternal desert, and will be swept along in the flood
and split at the capital, one part leading to the Vale of Hinnom
which is called Hell, and the other to the Gate of Mercy.

Notes to the Poem

The term for Hell in Hebrew, *Gehennom* or *Gehenna*, is derived from the Vale of Hinnom, traditionally located in Jerusalem and thought to be a site of ancient pagan child sacrifice. The Gate of Mercy is one of the ancient passages through the walls of Jerusalem's Old City.

Ten

Ten years since the Yom Kippur War,
and I'm sitting on a bench in the neighborhood, watching
my youngest son as he rides back and forth
on his bike. The old men make their way to the synagogue,
for these are the ten days of repentance; the poplars
by the school doors are so tall and my son
flashes back and forth among them. Why ten commandments,
I hear a child ask, and the answer is one for each
of the ten martyrs, but what would my answer be
on these days of repentance beneath a mild sun,
on a bench in the neighborhood, and my son riding
back and forth grasping the handlebars
with his ten fingers.

Notes to the Poem

The ten days of repentance fall between the Jewish new year (Rosh Hashanah) and the Day of Atonement (Yom Kippur).

A Poem of Grafts

I have to write about my life,
even on a lovely winter's day
after the rain, I have to chronicle
something besides a shoot from the soil
or twitter of birds among the pines
in the Jerusalem forest, I have to recall
the summer as well, the one before
the war that brought judgment and in which
we hoped to find atonement, the summer
I spent on the sand far from Jerusalem,
on the beaches of Sinai, in a tent with my wife.
I want to reconstruct the brightness,
I want to draw from the depths of fact
The Gulf of Eilat is very deep—
its depth reaches 1830 meters
below sea level (Dr. Menashe Har-El,
The Gulf of Eilat and Its Hidden Treasures)
what is stored like brain coral in the memory,
my wife coming slowly from the sea
in a tiny bathing suit that shines
almost painfully on her tanned curves,
her hips approaching like the horizon,
and I feel only the sweet heaviness
of my love for my wife and my world
The Jewish people's claim to the gulf
was established three millennia ago
when King Solomon, with vision and daring, built
his port in the wilderness of Etsion-Gever
(*The Gulf of Eilat and Its Hidden Treasures*)
and at the touch of her body I knew
that my life has meaning, that I have a world,
that I have a woman with whom I lie

passing my hand over her treasures
abundant like silent coral in the depths
of memory, and surely I already knew
there on the shore of the Red Sea
that I was finally a free man, privileged
to enjoy his possession of tent and wife
if you erase the Jewish soul in a child
you take away the essence of his humanity
(Yitzhak Katzenelson, *Vittel Diary*)
to stretch out in the shade of his tent
and play with the golden clasp fastened
upon her tanned back, and she breathes
and the clasp tightens and loosens with the perfume
that rises before my eyes, and I open
the gold link to free her breasts
the structure of the shore with its various parts
is different: steep granite cliffs
with small, narrow-mouthed rivers
creating the narrowest strip of sand
(*The Gulf of Eilat and Its Hidden Treasures*)
and her brimming hips as if there were
no place to rest beside them without touching,
loving their silkiness turned brown from all
her peregrinations on the sand, from sun
to shade, from shade to hands seeking
hungrily to liberate that hidden source
of life from which our children would bud
upon the Red Sea shore,
born from love set free in our tent,
my wife stretching out with a faint sigh
It is the way of pleasure to come after sorrow . . .
for it is not encountered without prior loss
(R. Yosef Albo, *The Book of Principles*)
and such love will not occur only once,

the desire of woman will not burn out,
will stay hid in the tent in the shade of the Sinai
which they decreed that we abandon
after the war that was alleged
to have fulfilled our need for atonement
and thus will the salvation and success of the nation
come only after the nation reaches
the fullest extent of its degradation,
which is like loss (The Book of Principles)
for thus were children born to us
at the shore of the Red Sea, new children
of freedom, whose bright swimsuits we shed
to bring their beauty out to the light,
who would live in the land of the covenant sublime
and, one day in the future, would see
only freedom from the heights of Jerusalem
they asked about my wife and children
who weren't with me—I said they were dead . . .
shall I tell them that my sons and their mother
have been led astray to a place from which
they will not return? (Vittel Diary)
Their tanks were distributed by platoons of three
tanks each along the line and were sited
in close support to the fortifications to deal
with any possible breakthrough between them
(Chaim Herzog, *The War of Atonement*)
for I want to see the future in Jerusalem,
and I created a future with my children who are free
as all that was born to us on the shore of Sinai
seeing voices and hearing kisses
in the tent, as the sea of our freedom cleanses
the sandy hem and the sun leans down
and the moon caresses your bronzed skin
until it shines like coral in the depths of memory
They will not love us . . . we're not bloodthirsty.

We're innocent of all bloodshed and hatred.
Therefore they despise us! (Vittel Diary)
I will always love this memory of your body,
will always want to promise a future
to our children, just as I did then
The attack was mounted along the entire front.
Contrary to Israeli estimates, but as Raful Eytan
had suggested, the main breakthrough point
was the Rafid opening (The War of Atonement)
and I was called to war in those days,
to Rafid, the main breakthrough point
There is grave danger in inquiring into principles,
for what is a heretic but one who denies
that something is a principle? (The Book of Principles)
and I was called to war in those days,
to Rafid, the main breakthrough point
through which broke the enemy whose desire was to destroy
the freedom that we learned on the shores of Sinai,
and I hated war in those days
We stopped loving each other, the feeling
of soul for soul ceased; what's worse—
there died as well in us our sense
of outrage for the disgrace of the human race . . .
if our love grew dull, then our hatred for evil
stopped altogether (Vittel Diary)
hated war because I loved only
your body, and I paid no heed to the soul
or to our children born on the shores of Sinai
who will come one day to the land of the covenant,
to fight for our lives that have not ended,
like a bud that springs up and turns golden
and is harvested, and in the end becomes
part of the world like a portion of bread—
I have to write about my life.

Notes to the Poem

Katzenelson's *Vittel Diary* was a composition he wrote in Hebrew during his detention in France (see notes to "The Murdered Song," above). Albo's *Book of Principles* is a fifteenth-century work of philosophy.

Born in Diaspora

Why are we ruled by others, and not by ourselves?
The sigh of the sea, wave after wave in the news,
the primal sea hinted to foreign scholars
that god fought god until we were formed,
the Great Deeps and the Leviathan, but we
will walk in the name of the Lord our God, and why
should we enthrone strangers? I remember a quiet shore
in the tropics of America, where I walked
after my father's death, on the sand smooth
till the line of the foam, and not seeing
the whole expanse, up to the end of the land, I went down
toward the waves, to feel salty drops
on my face that could not cry, for a Jew like me
won't cry, born in diaspora that isn't
exile, and so I reached the blind strip
and I heard a sound in the foam like bells,
and I saw sparkles of silver like a faded crown,
wave after wave of discarded cans, once filled with
cheap drinks, and now rusting in the deep.

Notes to the Poem

This translation is by Yehudit Ben-Yosef.

Protest Poem

It's easier to expose flaws than to cover them.
This truth testifies to the nature of reality
both around us and in the heart; it's easier to reprove
a man for an obvious fault than it is to prove
that a source of hidden beauty flows inside him, rising
and breaking on the austere shore. We are all dry land
molded by the sea of knowledge. But words
about the land of our fathers sound hollow to those
whose souls despise both land and sea,
a protest poem in their mouths and feathers at their ankles.
I saw their voices even in the hilly district
my heart desired to inhabit; peace, peace
they call out from the blue and the cloud's fringes blush,
peace from the tower's curtains, and there's nothing
in their hollow voices but injustice to others. I bent over
to examine the small abode of a snail on the slope,
among the fragrant shrubs, on the side of a rock.
Apparently from within its spirals it tried to reach
the high line of the Flood
and since then mutely whitened. Indeed, like the snail,
who was hurt to give our fathers the blue of the commandments,
I wait for the covering waters of knowledge.

Notes to the Poem

   This translation is by Yehudit Ben-Yosef.

A Greater Land of Israel

When I first heard the word *shalem*, or whole,
I thought it meant *shalom*, or peace, on the kibbutz
and in the country for maybe two months, at the beginning
of winter that returned with hints of narcissus and anemones
whose names I didn't yet know, mud-spattered and late
I came in from the fields to the dining room
and an elderly member asked, did you work the whole
day? Because at that time I'd only just started,
not as a man of words but as a man of the earth,
working in an orchard under the Syrian hills that jut out
along the Jordan River, and opposite the silent
summits of Lebanon in the north, I planted
citrus trees there, in the dust of the Hula Valley,
black, pure, without stains of malaria, for those
workers who simply work, who without words
spoke their intention to maintain the whole land of Israel,
and the Syrians fired from the ridge, bullets and
shells. Then you did a whole day's work, said
the elderly member from the generation that had drained the swamps,
and I remembered the young tree in my hand, the fragile
neck destined for splendor, whose roots I had watered,
and I said yes, for that day they hadn't fired
and to all that came my way I called *shalom*.

Notes to the Poem

This translation is by Yehudit Ben-Yosef.

To Cast Off My Burden, 1993

❧

In the Shade of a Tree

"No!" cried the woman and beat the air
that passed like a whisper over the open grave. "If,"
said the young man with the orders in his hand, still
stunned by the news. "Undoubtedly," explained
the government spokesman, pointing to the maps.
"Nonsense," pronounced the old man sitting in the park
in the shade of a tree, millions of leaves rising
to the sky.

In the Forest

In a world that kills to protest death
what hope is there for dreams? A thread
of budding leaves along a path in the forest.
In the heart of creation doomed by its nature,
what will the future deem? Thorns trampled in the summer
where the path continues, waiting for the first rain,
a heavy bombardment falling to melt the earth.
Ants hurry home. Every footstep leaves
a dreaming trace in the soft soil, and flowers
bloom in the spring.

Purim 1991

Why masks on Purim, a victory celebration?
Since the queen of the land of eternity grasped the golden
scepter stretching out like an oil pipeline from India
to Ethiopia, from Voholin to Brooklyn, from Meshed to Fez
we've worn masks as if every day were Purim,
we've celebrated a victory as if dumb luck were blessed,
a moment's random chance a metaphor for masked freedom,
and those legs sinking in the mire, those supplicating hands,
they belong to an image we brought with us from the exile,
Purim Entertainers by Yankel Adler of Lodz,
a refugee from the Shoah who painted heaven on earth
and earth in hell, a painting that I saw in the museum
where our people's declaration of independence was signed,
finally in our own homeland, staring down the fate
of exile among the nations, saying here
is our land for eternity and a new sanctuary
for that painting, a home of clean marble, since
in the old location there remains only what we wore,
more masks, for gas, this Purim 1991.

Notes to the Poem

In addition to a number of biblical and midrashic references to the Book of Esther, commemorated by Jews during the masquerade holiday of Purim, the poem refers to the gas masks that Israelis had to wear while under threat of biological and chemical attack from Iraq during the first Gulf War.

We Were Satisfied and We Remained, 1996

ও

Discoveries of Memory

The ancient page of the poem is full of holes.
So declared the scholar of poetry and tried
to reconstruct   nightingale and swift
sang to him night and day through the windows
      that were never
          shut
and the ancient page was also part of a rebirth
they sat there   page and scholar
and tried to reconstruct. And the poem's real owner
remained outside, walking to the woods, leaning
against a wall, stepping slowly and heavily like a camel
in the desert of the world, full of sand and pebbles
that fell from what?   Did something explode?
Who joined the sea to the mountain to the land
flowing with honey and the voice of the nightingale
and the swift   that exults
      in skies of ancient song

Tonight in the dream I saw: the world filling up
like a book, pages of that speech beyond the mountaintop,
or like a shoreline, an area for swimming and talk
and the grains of sand extending like a police barricade
that won't break under the pressure of the downtrodden,
won't withdraw from hopeful flags with nothing
new in them but the flash of an arm of a drowning man,
calling to the smiling sunbathers from his white-capped wave,
or like someone almost finished reading a book
who can't change the final pages, the falling columns
that utter words about the final splendor of those
buildings   that property
in a world filling up and if only the majority were with me
reading and rereading a book, certain as the drowning man
that its end will draw me home, but will a house in a dream
still stand by day? A book of ash whispered in the dark,
burnt in disappointment, a shoreline flattened
under the pounding of the waves, when only the hiss
of the foam recalls from the clefts of the season's end
the smiles of sunbathers, a hand leafing through the script
of the dream of someone whose exodus and return left him
abandoned in the land, before a world filling up
until there's no room, in a night that's almost over

The grass quivers in the wind of the Creator, a wind
created by the Creator of worlds to send Adam
walking on the grass in Eden   a vanished
garden. The wind trembles over a flower
that blooms amid the grass for a thirsty man,
so that he will stop and feast on beauty.   Far off
the field returns like a memory as evening makes its entrance
on the stage of our world, neither day nor night, Adam
will stand and know.   Know what?
And now ploughmen, the whole field a path
that leads back to Eden, for the ploughmen
demand a return to Eden, grandchildren will go,
a granddaughter will dance and a great-granddaughter
will make love in the quivering grass
                    that the Creator of worlds
in the wind   and I say
evening brings a grave as well to Adam, in the grass
he falls silent, a vast evening, not day and certainly not
night, for at night one sees the end,
and upon the dark vault blooms the gold
of the high priest

Within far-off Jerusalem voices call
one to the other make way make way
for straight through the desert is a path
from the biblical heavens to our talmudic earth
distant voices call one to the other
one from a wall to the Western Wall one
in the heart of the square filled with signs
and if only the ones assigned to rule had ears to hear no
and if only the police at the crossroads were resigned no
for one path to another and a road to its mate bring
evil to Jerusalem Zion blaring with triumphal noise from all
the voices calling in the wilderness make way and go forth
far off   one to the other
and the land is lined with traffic dotted to the temple mount
     in Jerusalem

It can happen
    likely
        to compare a dagger
            smooth and sharp
                and our sabbath
                stars
            six sides
        turning in hope
      waiting forever
if justice isn't done

Not manna   flowers of day
          in the president's vase
And across from the president's house outside
wandering birds   you ask
          not quail
not tranquil the president   in a house not his
          when he is president he is hated
          and his wandering crown protected by police
not upon the president   but the third
          temple

a young couple on the beach of their homeland until
the new moon   the escape   from a night
beneath a flashing sky a young couple
an eternal embrace amid the sound of the rolling waves
on the flat sand   grains
until the new moon. His face upon her shining breasts
grace and satisfaction, calling to the government of night
no! The government of day is strong, and so
they've set up a hut on the sand. Government of the sun
and they only embrace in the hut. But here
in the night among moons his hands are taught
to destroy and to touch the tender essence of her thighs
his face upon her bold breasts, until moonless
until no fear of the government of the dagger

fragments around
                    so he said
whose mouth
                    in the earth
still speaks
                    to whomever listens
lest it be broken
            before an orphaned wall and a burnt roof

And what will be destroyed when missiles rain upon our capital
the enormous stones the house the fire penetrated with
flame and shattering, everything we didn't discover
burnt   in disappointment
our roofs like the skies of the Western Wall
noons of emptiness
a book with no beginning, interpreted like a ruin, dust
if we don't stand, if we don't rise from the shore
if we don't raise up our hands waving in hope
to the ceiling of our land, events of God
who gives according to what we take, under stars
for we were like the sand of the sea and now stars
on the length of the Western Wall our flags in the wind
two azure bands like the length of the courtyard
six points of day or a thousand until the coming
of sabbath within them

The page torn from the book, he said, told
what will not be done. For if it were done
there would be no one   to tell
in a voice twisting like a song on a festival night
        that it will not be finished
        in our world
a forgotten page, mute as hieroglyphs
in the depths   of heaven
and they call along the shore as they write in Jerusalem
interpreting the future, after Purim and its thrills
after the wound of the exodus to freedom, they will sit
the reader and the writer together to close the rift
beneath firework skies of an independence day
that will join the sea to the mountain to the land
and continue on to join to the festival
                        discoveries of memory

Notes to the Poem

This dense and complex poem enacts in its very form—which includes biblical features and modernist fragmentation—the challenge of maintaining meaning and continuity that it so anxiously treats. Sections are made to look like fragments of an ancient text, with holes and lacunae, that demand some perhaps impossible reconstruction. The import is as political and spiritual as it is literary. Ben-Yosef, against the background of the rending political debates over the Oslo process (the poem dates from the first half of the 1990s), fears what will become of a Jewish society that can no longer read the text of itself, that can no longer discern "a path / from the biblical heavens to our talmudic earth." What Ben-Yosef means by this is not some narrowly theocratic understanding of Zionism or the state of Israel. The title of the poem informs us of his desire for a dialectical integration of the past and the present, the old and the new informing each other. When this is not done, one experiences the "government of the dagger," a text defaced with holes that allow for no new, restorative reading. What is needed is an outlook "that will join the sea to the mountain to the land"—the global and the spiritual and the political in a conscious whole.

Aging Lion

Behind a lattice of blades of grass
that stir with ants, in my stony lair
only memories dare approach
your hair, a sun clouded by despair.
I miss the chirping bird that flew,
and I ask for an aging lion's due.

In poems I compared your thighs
to roots, your hips' curve to the rose.
Will this perfection pass away?
Both books and people decompose.
Time bends our spines and cracks our glue,
so I ask for an aging lion's due.

And are you without any fear at all?
In dreams do you still hear my roar?
Take pity on these orphaned jaws
that devoured prey once but now are sore,
a sentence only sweetened by you.
Please, give an aging lion his due.

Notes to the Poem

This poem looks back at the much earlier sequence of "Songs for Yehudit."

For the Sake of Our Land

The word for "life" is always plural in Hebrew,
as if the Jew had several lives, as it was said
of the divine blooming of our father in Eden,
the father of humanity: *and God breathed
into his nostrils the breath of life*, or "lives"
in Hebrew, two worlds, which disappears in English,
for a man lives fully only in our tongue,
even a young man, who is also in love
in this garden, lording it over tree and stone
like one of the mountains, arriving fresh in the morning
at the gate of stones to pass along the lane,
the millions of needles of cedar and cypress above
his head, a young woman at his side trembling
with dew, he kisses her hand with mock chivalry
for he doesn't follow old folks' customs,
and the land is beautiful, and again the woman lifts
her eyes to him beseeching him to delight
in her body blooming like a divine flower beneath
the cedar, the cypress and the pine, the path of needles,
for the love of life leads to the love of God,
and only excess of death can hide His image.

And how does the land respond? In youthful love
it blooms for them, millions of needles, crocus
in winter, poppy in spring, grass on whose tips
the man lay in tender delight with his woman,
his love weightier than stone and light as a spirit
hovering over her charms as if strolling on his estate
where he will stay for the rest of his life, or his lives
in Hebrew, for there lives in him still the young man
who sows in his girl's beauty the purity of the crocus,
the father who soothes his wife with the poppy's flame,
the old man recalling it all, facing the stones.

A field of weeping: the place nearby where women
sit and lament, a field neither planted nor sown
and whose dust is pure, like that young man who kissed
the hand of his girl and ran toward the fire.
A field of weeping, may we be faithful to its stones,
and beware the field of corpses whose dust defiles
as lands outside the land of Israel defile
by touch and by yearning, unlike our land, pure
as the crocus and fiery as the poppy, the young man
had no field of corpses, no bones, no bonus, no prize,
only his beloved's hand, and happily she lies
down with him upon the land he loves,
on that divine day, with both of his lives.

Yet why did He say *and I will remember the land*,
when we were in the lands of exile whose dust
defiles? Why did He say *and I will remember
the covenant of the ancestors*, and the land trembles
with dew in a needle's shadow, and why did some
young men hold fast to a handful of specks, the buds
of crocus and poppy, to kiss like a baby her body,
all her beauty, as woman and mother, alive,
walking in the land of their rest for the rest of their lives,
for it is their house, a field of weeping too,
a place where an old man sees his loved ones
as if through the dust, beneath cedar and cypress,
and the gate of stones, for here is the house,
behold: for the sake of our land, voices rise up
all around saying, and I will remember
the land, the pure ground of that resting place
of all life—please may they live forever.

Notes to the Poem

This poem deals with the murder of a young Jewish couple at
the time that the Nobel Peace Prize was awarded to Yasir Arafat and

Yitzhak Rabin. Ben-Yosef puns darkly on the Talmudic phrase *beit hapras* (possibly meaning house of the shattering, or house of the scattering), which refers in rabbinic law to an area in which one suspects there may be a grave or buried corpses scattered, but which could be creatively mistranslated as "house of the prize." In the original, Ben-Yosef uses the term and observes that the murdered young man had neither house nor prize.

Between Holy and Profane, 1999

❦

Aliyah

Rabbi Ovadiah of Bertinoro
made a journey of two years
from Renaissance Italy to water the ruins
of Jerusalem with his tears.

On his way he stopped in the land of the Nile
and pored over old parchment
until his angels urged him on:
enough scholarly enlargement!

"In Jerusalem I've become a gravedigger,"
he wrote to his friends abroad,
for even among ruins his pen was glad
to sing of the land of God.

"In Jerusalem each and every wind
comes to sing His praise
before it turns and blows, refreshing
all who walk in His ways."

"In Jerusalem I have found not more
than seventy families of Israel,
so few in number, so great in need,
God willing we shall not fail."

In Italy he wrote his commentary
on the Mishnah—all of it.

Here, he dug graves for thirteen years
and was buried on Olivet.

His gravesite's one that I can't see,
though I sit here at the casement
open to the winds while my yearning heart
asks, how long such abasement?

Only one grave can I see from my door:
the tomb at Mount Nebo
of one who gazed at the Promised Land
before he had to go.

Notes to the Poem

Ovadiah of Bertinoro was an Italian rabbi who moved to Jerusalem in the late fifteenth century. He is known for his commentary on the Mishnah. He is buried on the Mount of Olives (Olivet). Mount Nebo is the location from where Moses is said to have been allowed to view the Promised Land, but not to enter it, before his death.

Poems Published Posthumously

In Memory of Reuven Ben-Yosef, 2002

✍

Lament

For whom is a lament? For those expelled
from their homes, from the beauty of the fields they tilled
in hopes that they would one day see fulfilled
the vision of peace for Israel that prophets foretold,
who raised a generation, and now each child
wants to know why they have become so reviled
by a crooked government that calls creation defiled
by innocent babes not even ten days old;
or perhaps the lament is rather for those who planned
the expulsion, agreed to do what our enemies demand,
uprooted the vineyard, lopped off the limbs of the land,
as if they heard and obeyed some infernal command.

And what does one lament? The uprooted seed,
the once thriving city now dismantled, emptied,
the cold wind blowing across the orphaned abode,
the charred branches that once allowed people to feed,
to absorb countless refugees in need,
the abandoned hotel, the lonely cement road;
or should one lament the rest of the country instead
where, as if on a platter, the houses are spread
invitingly and humbly below mountains of dread,
with paper-thin walls that are heavy as the dead.

The Main Thing

> All the world is a very narrow bridge, but the main thing is not to fear.
> —Rabbi Nachman of Bratslav

The main thing is not to fear, yet if the bridge,
that slender thread stretched out to eternity,
has snapped, and you are unable to edge
forward, stuck on that narrow, winding ridge,
the storm raging around as you cling to the ledge
and search in vain for a sign of heavenly pity,
and hear the world-abyss below you beckon--
if that is the main thing, then what comes second?

Poems Written in English

The Endless Seed, 1959

∽

From **The Artists Mourn Barry Fogelson**

Mourning is our weather now, the season
Green, the birds returned, tulips unrolled, but
Blackness is our seed now, and our spring.
Our farm lies fallow, while the farmers pray.
Others still ride the chariot of May,
Blind with speed, too dizzy to see reason
Record the missing soul no wheels could hold, but
Blackness is our seed now, and our spring.

We harvest stuff sustaining life: his bloom
Was gold with hope, cheering the belly's ache, but
Blackness is our seed now, and our spring.
We must burn weeds in silence, for this ground
Has lost him who would, by his plow, expound
Eternity, condense the year, untomb
Last autumn's leaves, torn by the worldly rake, but
Blackness is our seed now, and our spring.

Restoring youth, keeping the first shape pure,
He fought the red death settled on late trees, but
Blackness is our seed now, and our spring.
He visioned nations, crimson at their cores,
Bursting outward rotten spots of wars,
Destroying, doomed, while he had the cure
That soothed the leaf, to temper man's disease, but
Blackness is our seed now, and our spring.

Planting under hail, his chest was shield
To life, until his smile turned wild skies blue, but
Blackness is our seed now, and our spring.
He made man into cloud, to wind, to sea,
Crumbling, whirling, slashing misery,
Wounds his blood bore, while in his fertile field
Lush crops were born that, tasted, would renew, but
Blackness is our seed now, and our spring.

Our work this year shall be his monument,
To grieve his absence, breed against its cause, but
Blackness is our seed now, and our spring.
He saw, like Daniel, secrets of our dreams,
Slapped fault, sang fancy, praised what praise redeems,
Envigored hope, molded earth's merriment,
But knew no art to stop the lions' jaws, so
Blackness is our seed now, and our spring.

Sandcastles by the Sea

I watched the children frolic in the sand,
And now, if I bend over, I can see
The city which they worked, whose spires stand
Behind great walls to halt the enemy.
Here pebbly streets with offices and shops
Like lines on old cheeks wind throughout the town,
Where, lowly, I regard the castle tops,
And think how high the lords are, looking down.
Who knows what passions breathe within these towers
That young joy built, but left for elder thought?
I see a strong prince strut his youthful powers,
A princess kiss, and try to seem distraught,
And life is some wild love game to be played
Till waves take from me what the children made.

The Burning Bush

He looked ahead: the desert bore a green flame
Beneath the mountain; sky went white;
Wind silenced; out of absence came
The strong oration:
Moses, know you not of Israel's plight?

Slowing the sheep's pace
Moses nears the vision
Unfelt hands erase
His layman's indecision
And draw him, while he hides his face
And wonders how he found this place

He looked before him: bush was burned in red flame
Through which green leaves gleamed; sky spun black;
Wind thundered; louder than all came
The poignant question:
Know you not of whips on Israel's back?

Stroking the sheep still
Moses stands before fact
Unheard voices fill
His young mind with the old pact
And teach him, while fear's acids spill
Upon the pale wool of his will

He looked behind: the mountain swayed in gold flame
Over the blank sand; sky hazed blue;
Wind whispered; out of vagueness came
The huge concretion:
Know you not what force has summoned you?

Guiding the sheep's speed
Moses approaches grief
Unseen bodies bleed

For revival of belief
And beg him, while he shapes his deed
Out of the Lord Who knows all need

On a Photo of a Dance Figure of My Distant Beloved

You moving are the feathered tunes of spring
Come from an unknown south to soothe these snows,
Turn ice to air with song, caress with wing
Upraised the withered flower till it grows;
Leaping to live in warmth your breast brings forth,
Trees father troops of leaves to frighten wind;
While chilly clouds, cruel ogres of the north,
Shriek at your sun-lit hair and flee, chagrined.
Yet now you dance in fixity, and weather
Stays winter, flocks form zeros in arrest
Above my land's cold arms, which touch no feather
Of your high beauty, that should here take nest
Where I watch birds the lonely months suspend,
Hoping to hold them when their poses end.